Benjamin Franklin

written and illustrated by
Rod Espinosa

visit us at
www.abdopublishing.com

Published by Red Wagon, a division of the ABDO Publishing Group, 8000 West 78th Street, Edina, Minnesota 55439.

Printed in the United States.

Written and illustrated by Rod Espinosa
Colored and lettered by Rod Espinosa
Edited by Stephanie Hedlund
Interior layout and design by Antarctic Press
Cover art by Rod Espinosa
Cover design by Neil Klinepier

Library of Congress Cataloging-in-Publication Data

Espinosa, Rod.
Benjamin Franklin / written and illustrated by Rod Espinosa.
p. cm. -- (Bio-graphics)
Includes index.
ISBN 978-1-60270-066-6
1. Franklin, Benjamin, 1706-1790--Juvenile literature. 2. Statesmen--United States--Biography--Juvenile literature. 3. Scientists--United States--Biography--Juvenile literature. 4. Inventors--United States--Biography--Juvenile literature. 5. Printers--United States--Biography--Juvenile literature. 6. Graphic novels. I. Title.

E302.6.F8E86 2008
973.3092--dc22
[B] 2007004350

TABLE of CONTENTS

Chapter 1 Young Inventor

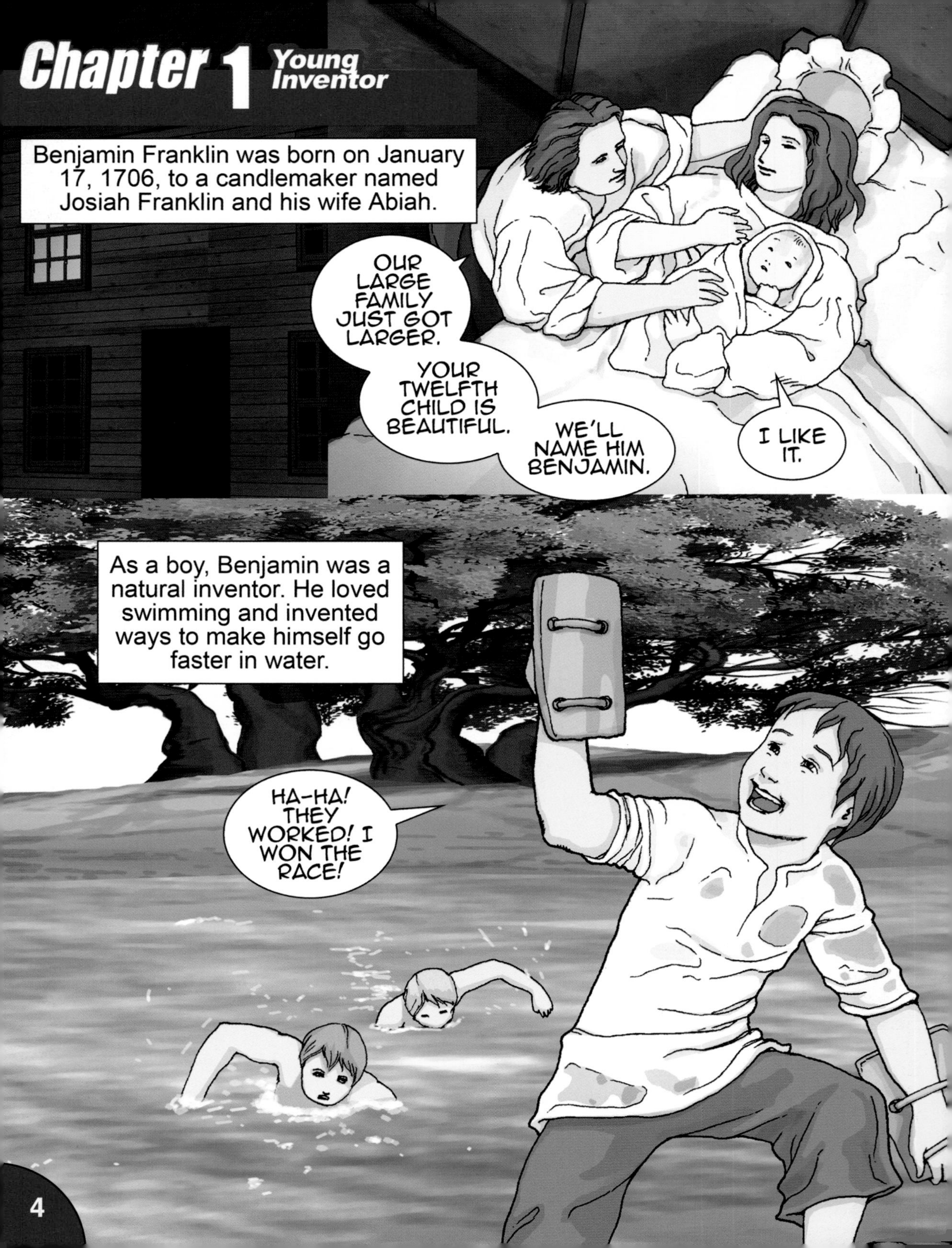
Benjamin Franklin was born on January 17, 1706, to a candlemaker named Josiah Franklin and his wife Abiah.
OUR LARGE FAMILY JUST GOT LARGER.
YOUR TWELFTH CHILD IS BEAUTIFUL.
WE'LL NAME HIM BENJAMIN.
I LIKE IT.
As a boy, Benjamin was a natural inventor. He loved swimming and invented ways to make himself go faster in water.
HA-HA! THEY WORKED! I WON THE RACE!

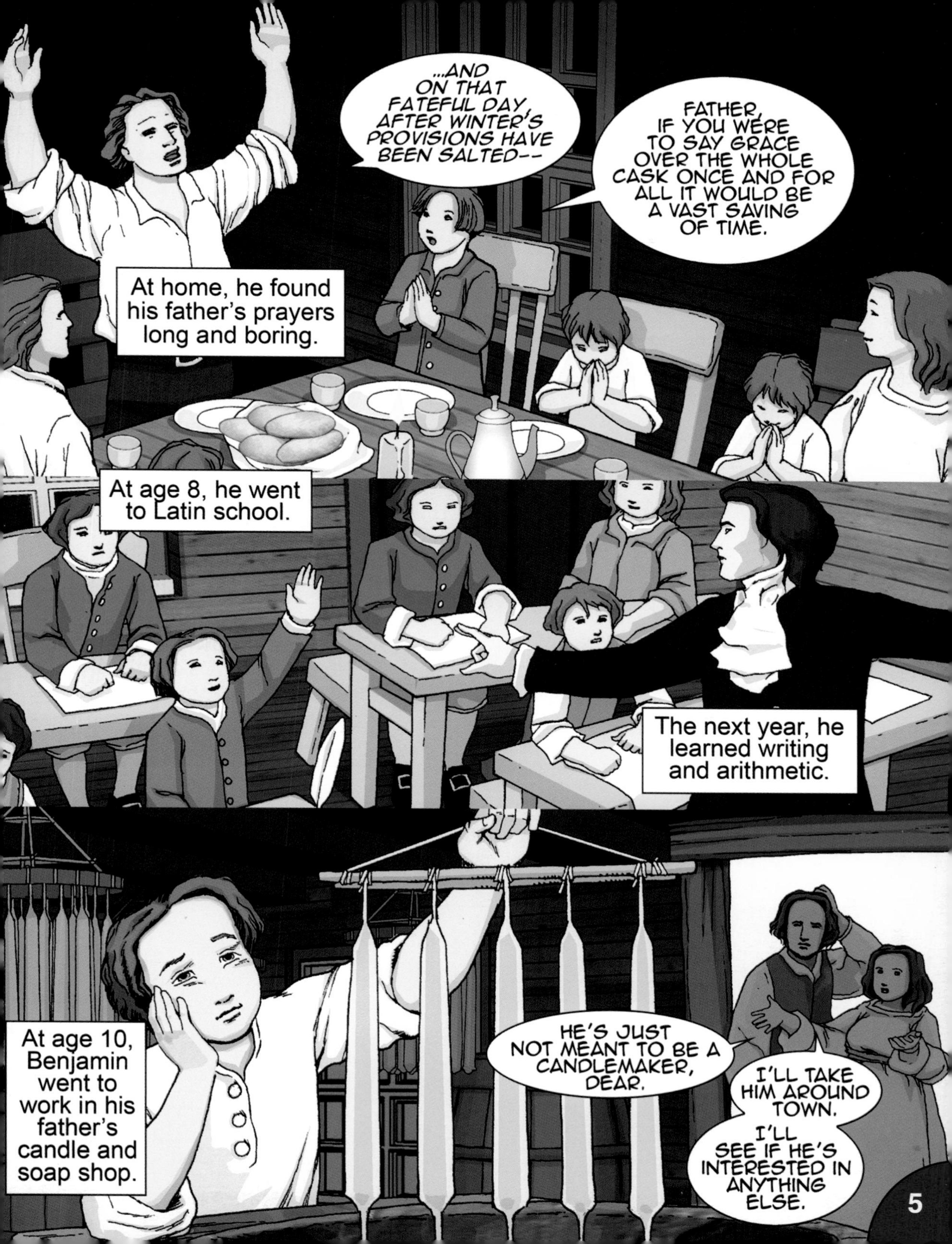

...AND ON THAT FATEFUL DAY, AFTER WINTER'S PROVISIONS HAVE BEEN SALTED--
FATHER, IF YOU WERE TO SAY GRACE OVER THE WHOLE CASK ONCE AND FOR ALL IT WOULD BE A VAST SAVING OF TIME.
At home, he found his father's prayers long and boring.
At age 8, he went to Latin school.
The next year, he learned writing and arithmetic.
At age 10, Benjamin went to work in his father's candle and soap shop.
HE'S JUST NOT MEANT TO BE A CANDLEMAKER, DEAR.
I'LL TAKE HIM AROUND TOWN.
I'LL SEE IF HE'S INTERESTED IN ANYTHING ELSE.

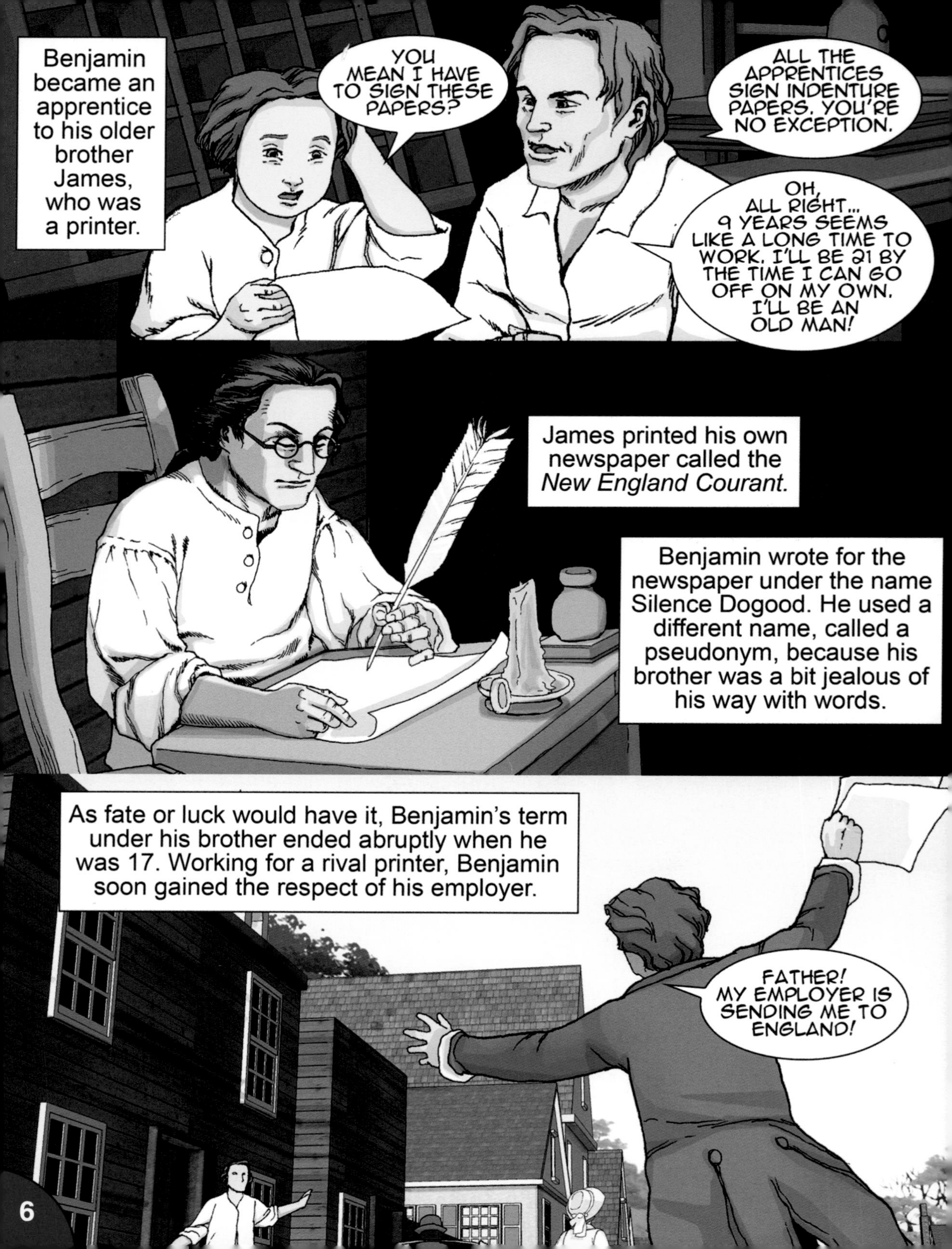

Benjamin became an apprentice to his older brother James, who was a printer.
YOU MEAN I HAVE TO SIGN THESE PAPERS?
ALL THE APPRENTICES SIGN INDENTURE PAPERS. YOU'RE NO EXCEPTION.
OH, ALL RIGHT... 9 YEARS SEEMS LIKE A LONG TIME TO WORK. I'LL BE 21 BY THE TIME I CAN GO OFF ON MY OWN. I'LL BE AN OLD MAN!
James printed his own newspaper called the *New England Courant*.
Benjamin wrote for the newspaper under the name Silence Dogood. He used a different name, called a pseudonym, because his brother was a bit jealous of his way with words.
As fate or luck would have it, Benjamin's term under his brother ended abruptly when he was 17. Working for a rival printer, Benjamin soon gained the respect of his employer.
FATHER! MY EMPLOYER IS SENDING ME TO ENGLAND!

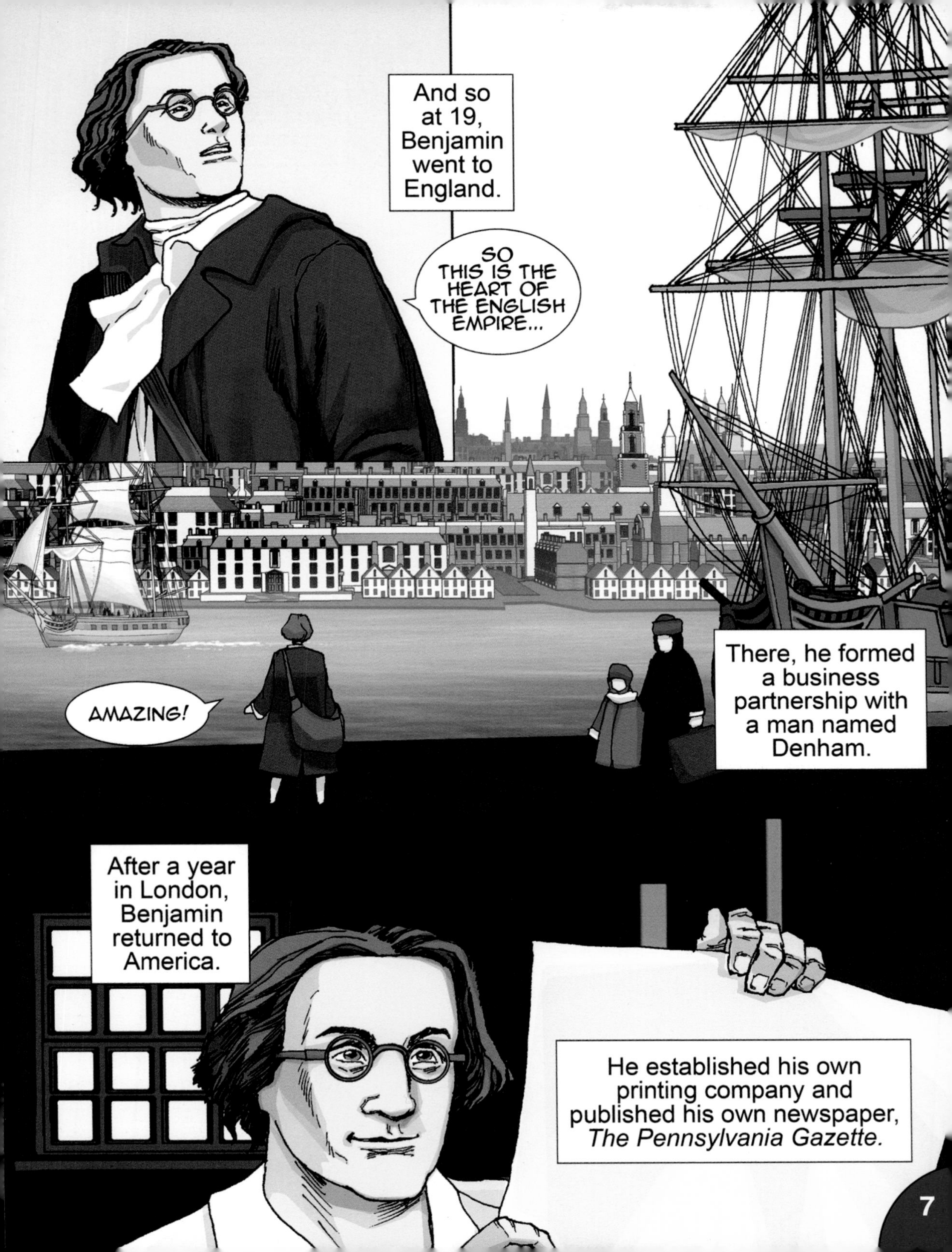
And so at 19, Benjamin went to England.
SO THIS IS THE HEART OF THE ENGLISH EMPIRE...
AMAZING!
There, he formed a business partnership with a man named Denham.
After a year in London, Benjamin returned to America.
He established his own printing company and published his own newspaper, *The Pennsylvania Gazette.*

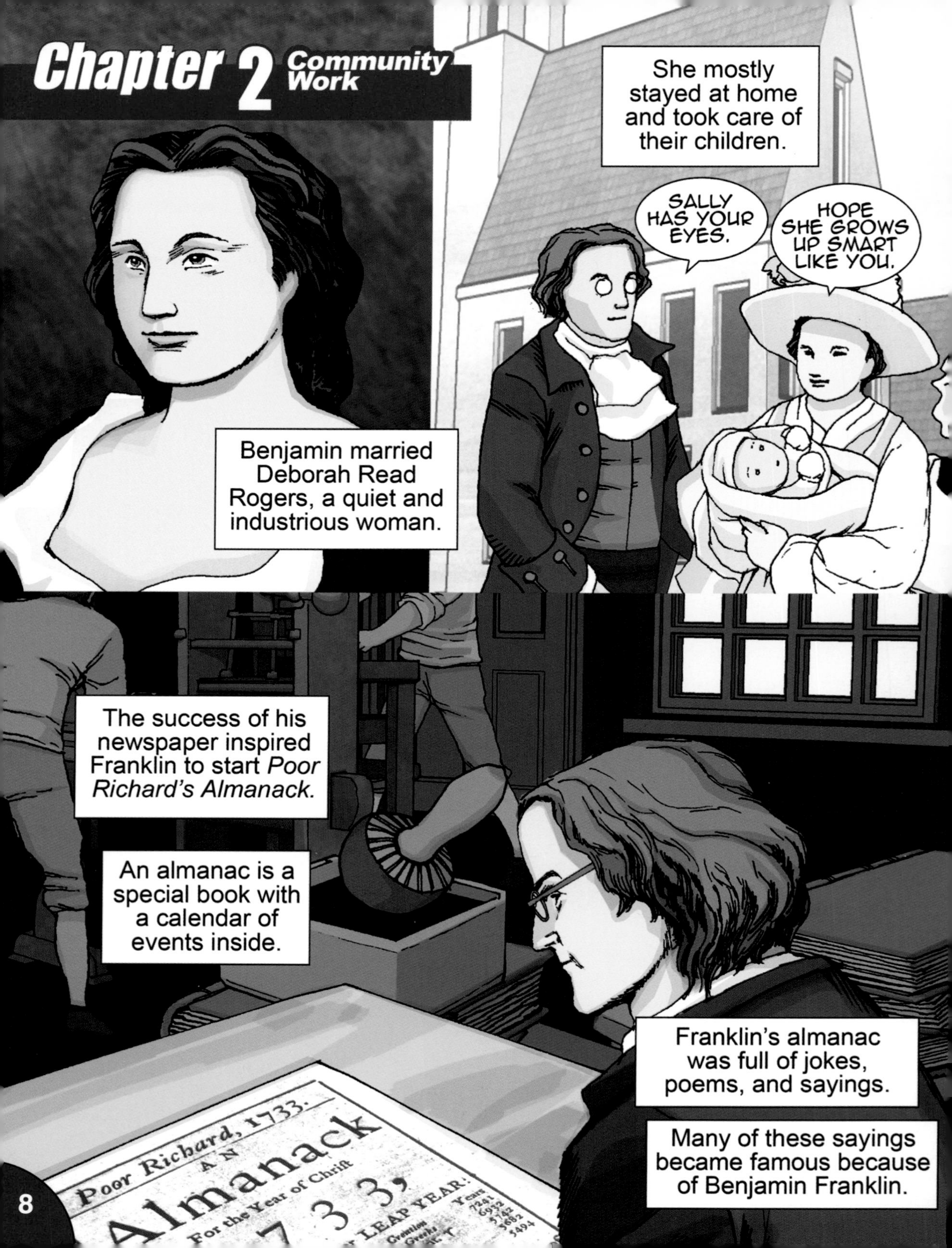
Chapter 2 Community Work
Benjamin married Deborah Read Rogers, a quiet and industrious woman.
She mostly stayed at home and took care of their children.
SALLY HAS YOUR EYES.
HOPE SHE GROWS UP SMART LIKE YOU.
The success of his newspaper inspired Franklin to start *Poor Richard's Almanack*.
An almanac is a special book with a calendar of events inside.
Franklin's almanac was full of jokes, poems, and sayings.
Many of these sayings became famous because of Benjamin Franklin.
Poor Richard, 1733.
AN
Almanack
For the Year of Christ
1733,
LEAP YEAR.

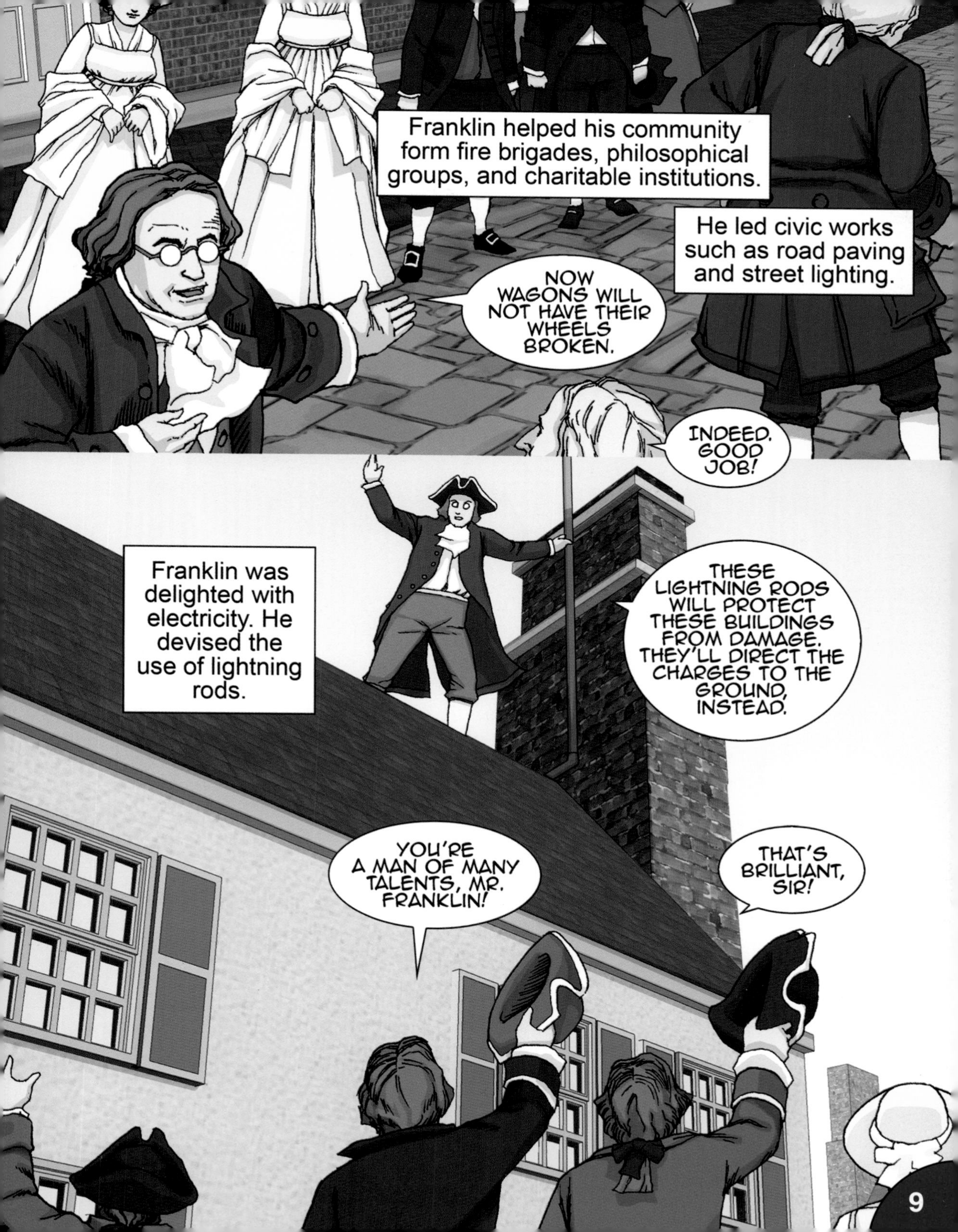
Franklin helped his community form fire brigades, philosophical groups, and charitable institutions.
He led civic works such as road paving and street lighting.
NOW WAGONS WILL NOT HAVE THEIR WHEELS BROKEN.
INDEED. GOOD JOB!
Franklin was delighted with electricity. He devised the use of lightning rods.
THESE LIGHTNING RODS WILL PROTECT THESE BUILDINGS FROM DAMAGE. THEY'LL DIRECT THE CHARGES TO THE GROUND, INSTEAD.
YOU'RE A MAN OF MANY TALENTS, MR. FRANKLIN!
THAT'S BRILLIANT, SIR!

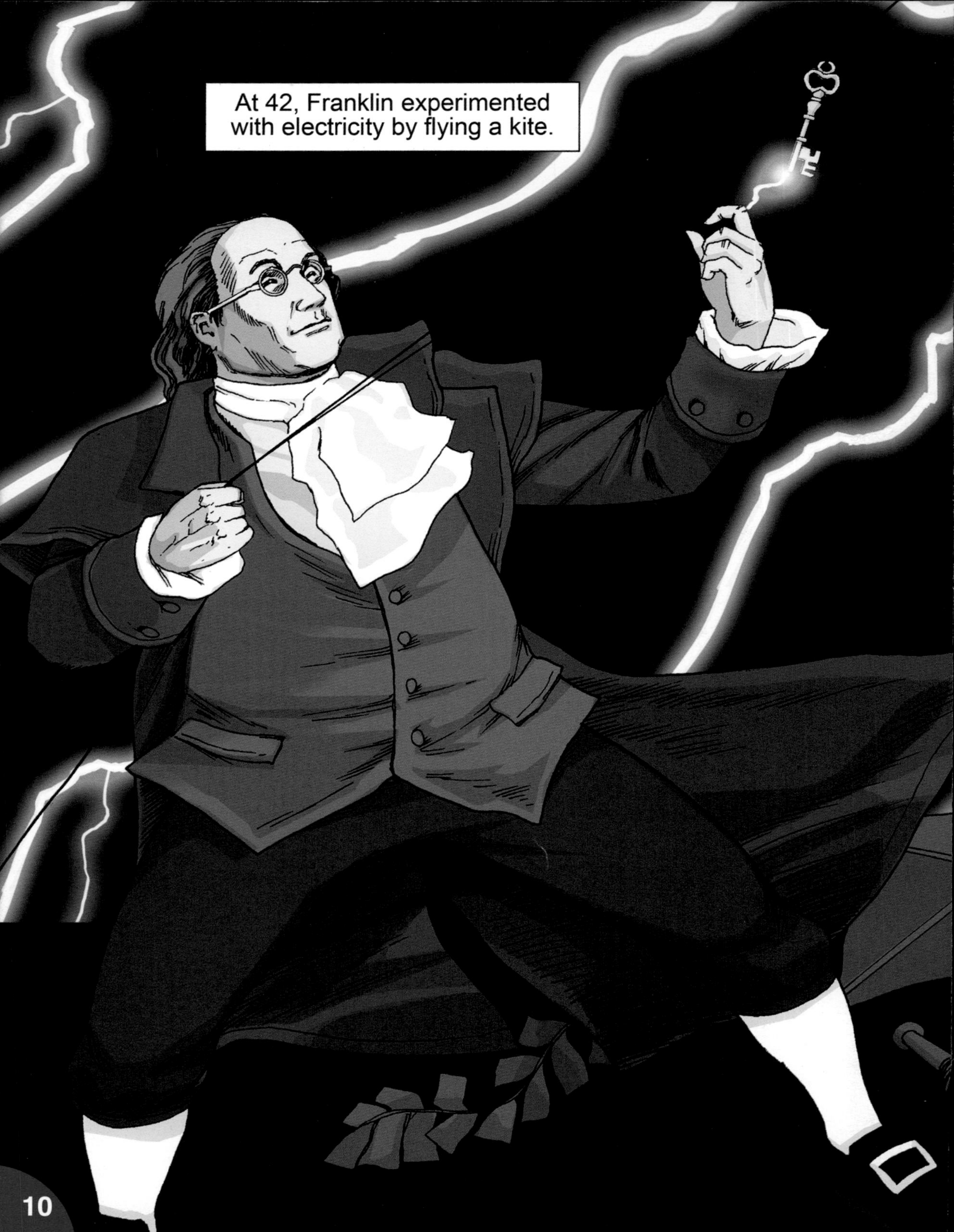
At 42, Franklin experimented with electricity by flying a kite.

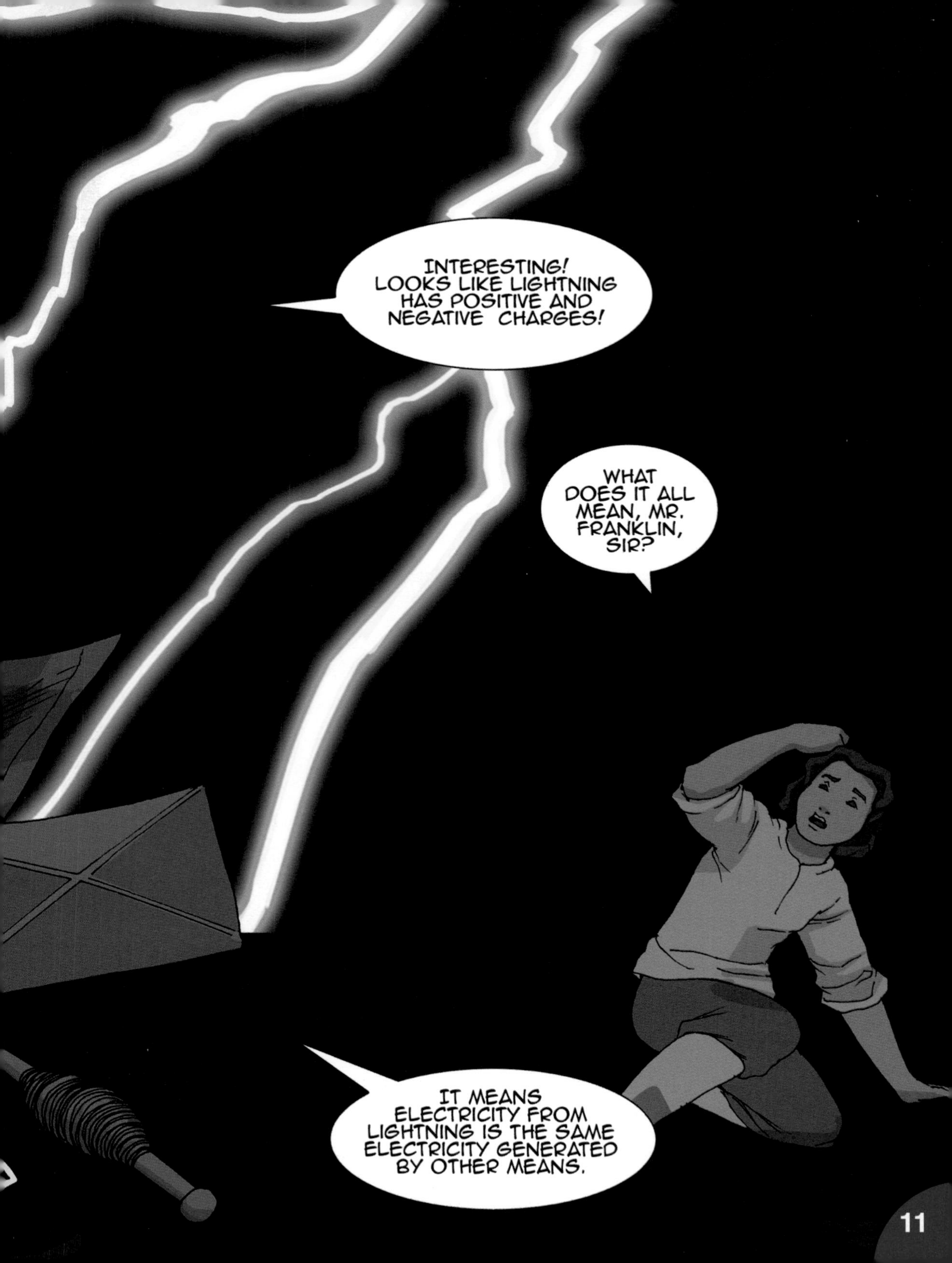
INTERESTING! LOOKS LIKE LIGHTNING HAS POSITIVE AND NEGATIVE CHARGES!
WHAT DOES IT ALL MEAN, MR. FRANKLIN, SIR?
IT MEANS ELECTRICITY FROM LIGHTNING IS THE SAME ELECTRICITY GENERATED BY OTHER MEANS.

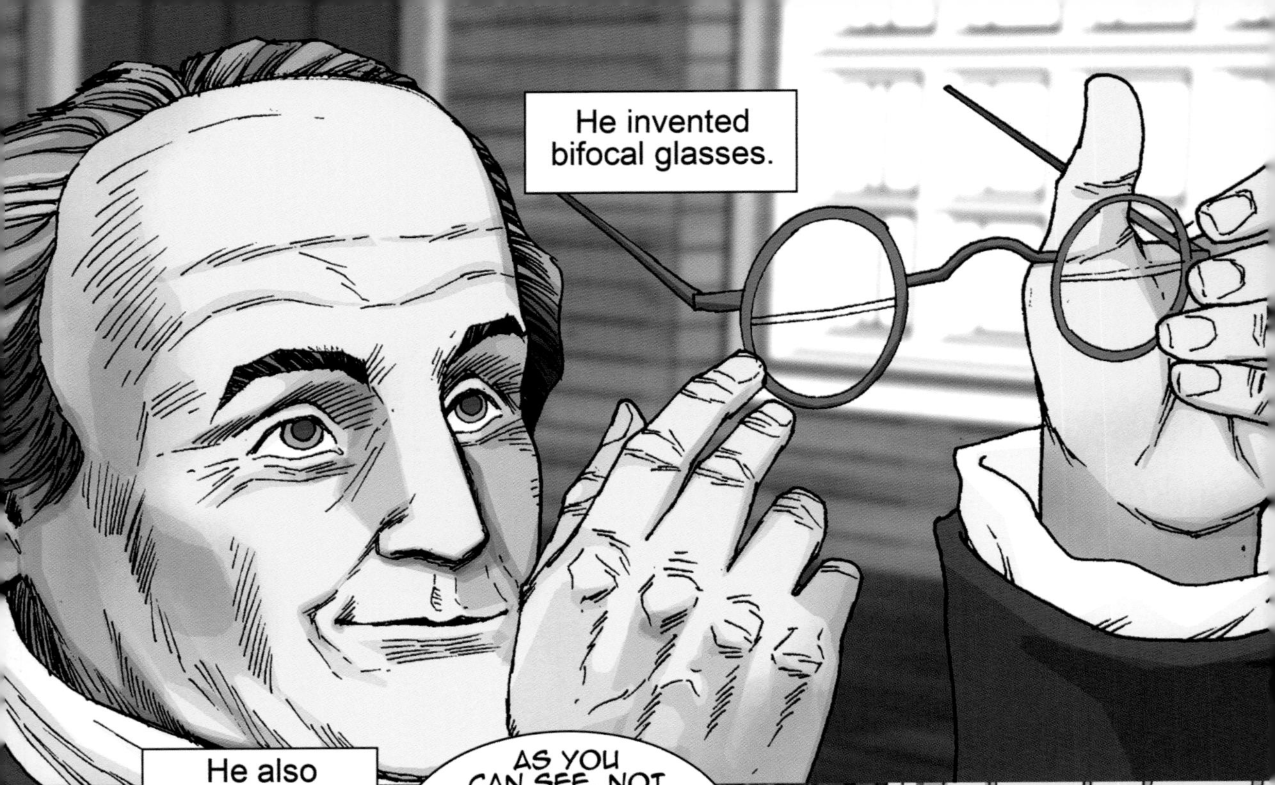
He invented bifocal glasses.

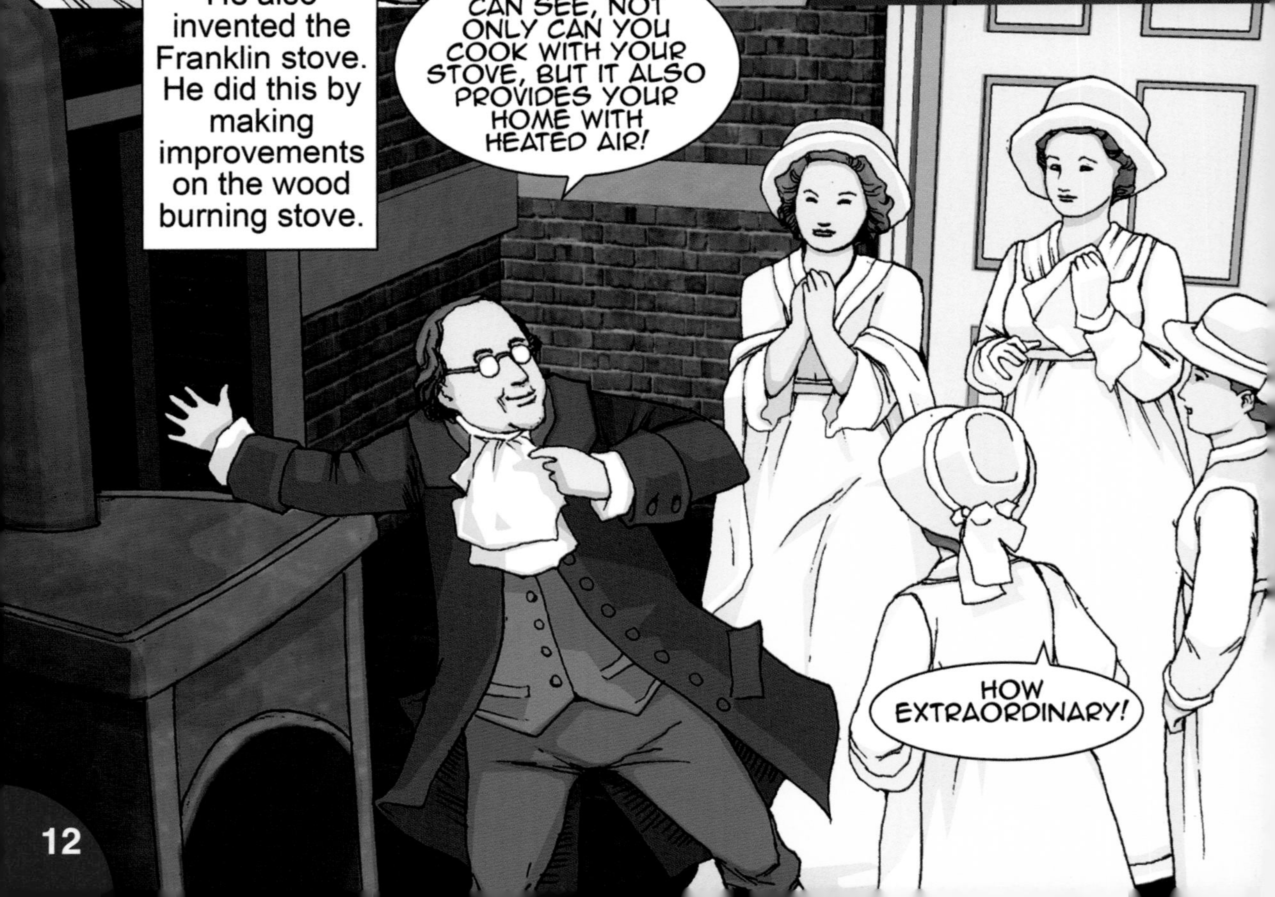
He also invented the Franklin stove. He did this by making improvements on the wood burning stove.
AS YOU CAN SEE, NOT ONLY CAN YOU COOK WITH YOUR STOVE, BUT IT ALSO PROVIDES YOUR HOME WITH HEATED AIR!
HOW EXTRAORDINARY!

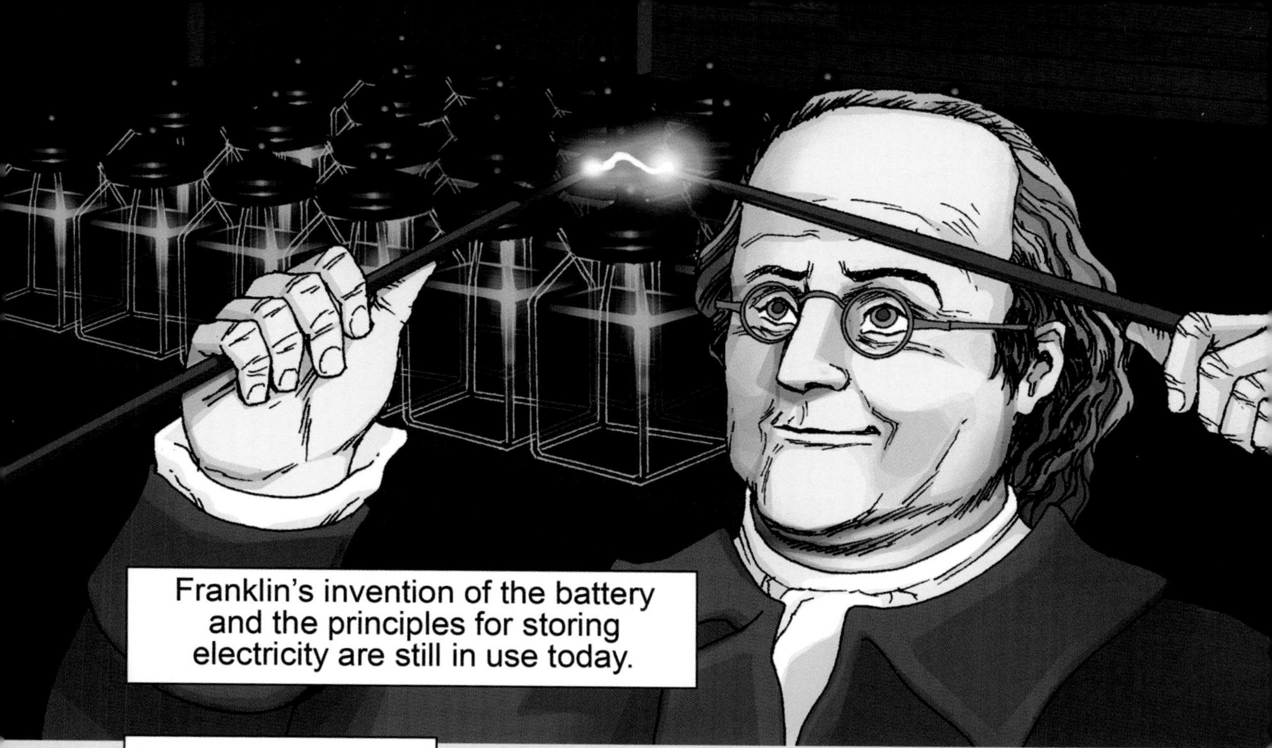
Franklin's invention of the battery and the principles for storing electricity are still in use today.

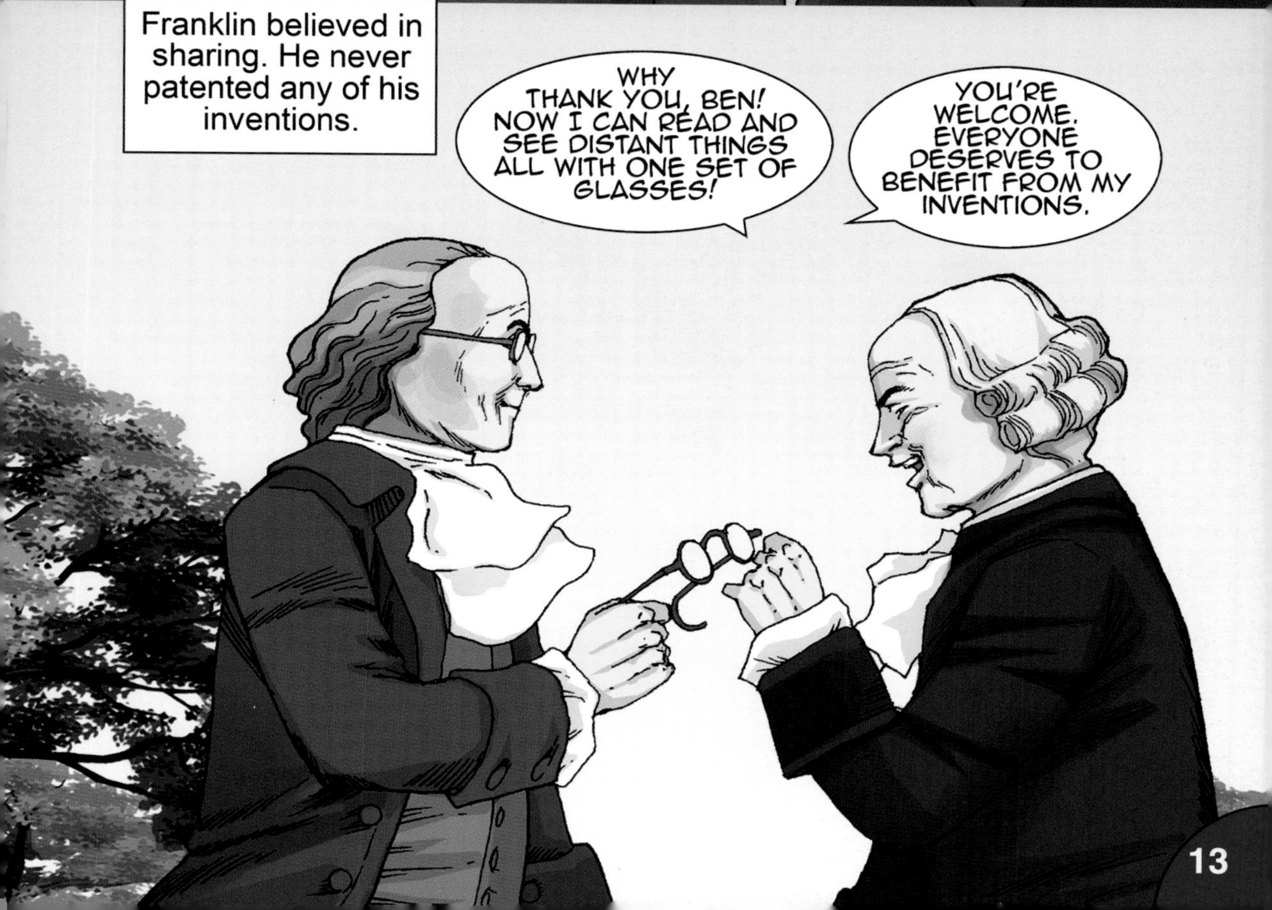
Franklin believed in sharing. He never patented any of his inventions.
WHY THANK YOU, BEN! NOW I CAN READ AND SEE DISTANT THINGS ALL WITH ONE SET OF GLASSES!
YOU'RE WELCOME. EVERYONE DESERVES TO BENEFIT FROM MY INVENTIONS.

Chapter 3 The Albany Plan

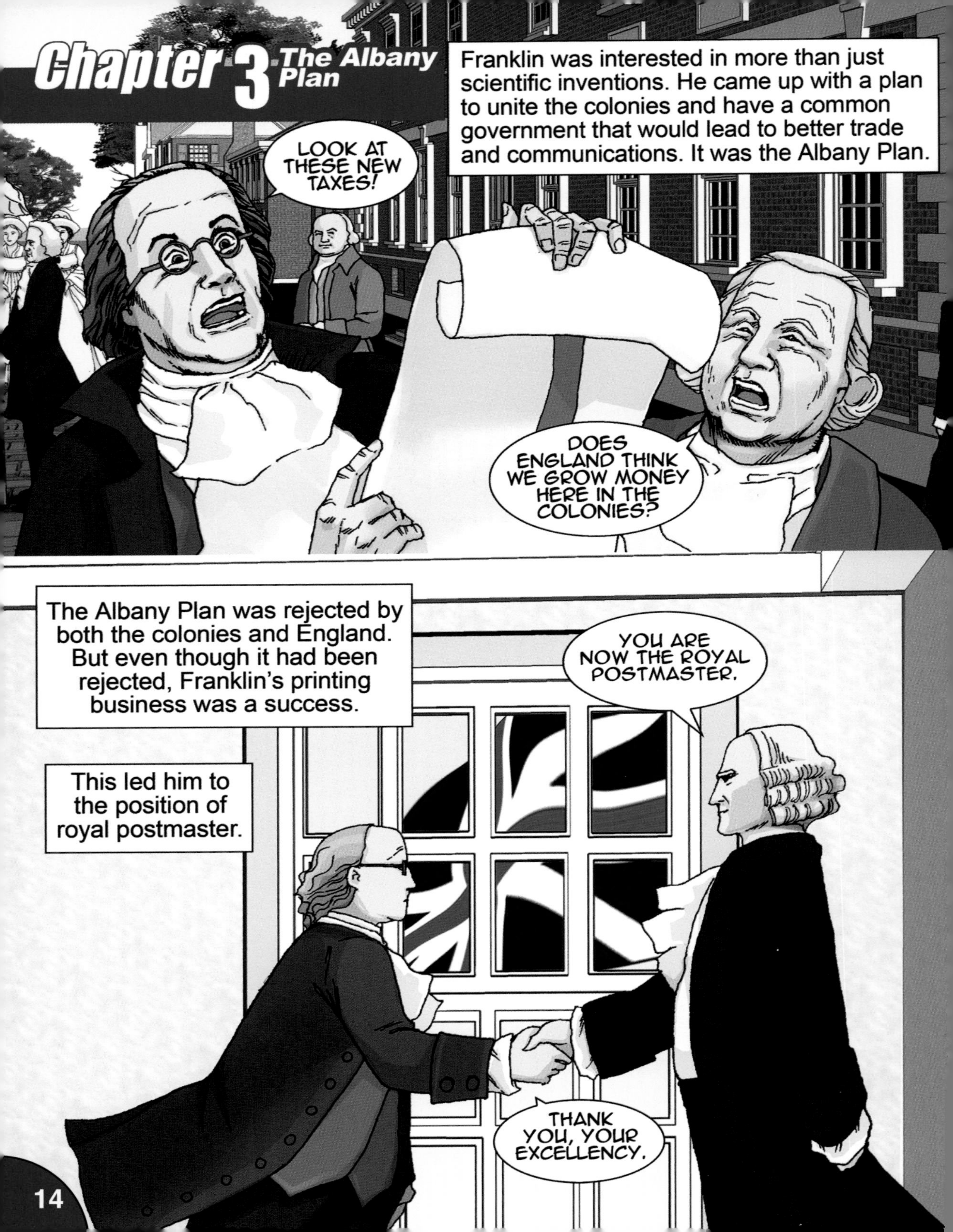

Franklin was interested in more than just scientific inventions. He came up with a plan to unite the colonies and have a common government that would lead to better trade and communications. It was the Albany Plan.
LOOK AT THESE NEW TAXES!
DOES ENGLAND THINK WE GROW MONEY HERE IN THE COLONIES?
The Albany Plan was rejected by both the colonies and England. But even though it had been rejected, Franklin's printing business was a success.
This led him to the position of royal postmaster.
YOU ARE NOW THE ROYAL POSTMASTER.
THANK YOU, YOUR EXCELLENCY.

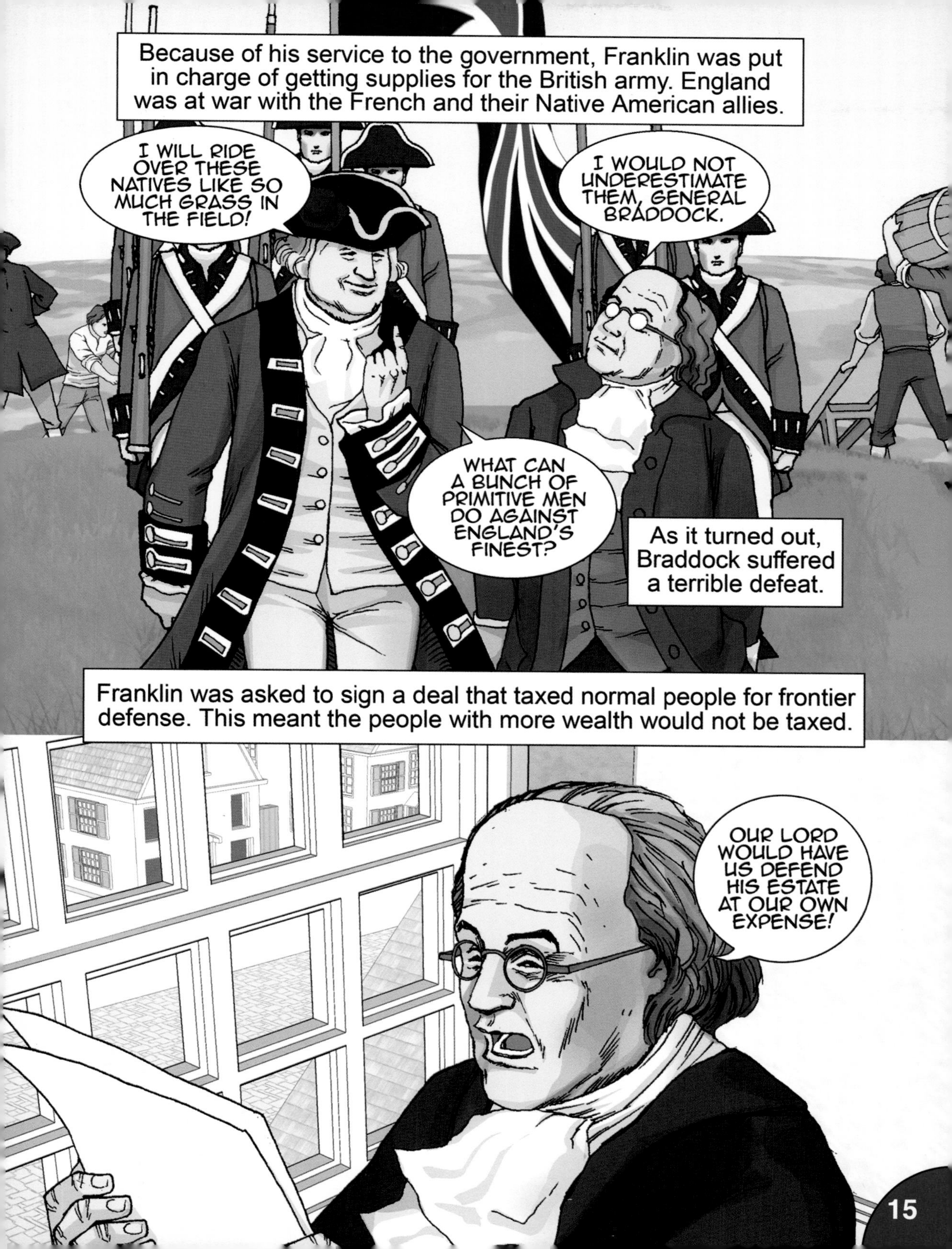
Because of his service to the government, Franklin was put in charge of getting supplies for the British army. England was at war with the French and their Native American allies.
I WILL RIDE OVER THESE NATIVES LIKE SO MUCH GRASS IN THE FIELD!
I WOULD NOT UNDERESTIMATE THEM, GENERAL BRADDOCK.
WHAT CAN A BUNCH OF PRIMITIVE MEN DO AGAINST ENGLAND'S FINEST?
As it turned out, Braddock suffered a terrible defeat.
Franklin was asked to sign a deal that taxed normal people for frontier defense. This meant the people with more wealth would not be taxed.
OUR LORD WOULD HAVE US DEFEND HIS ESTATE AT OUR OWN EXPENSE!

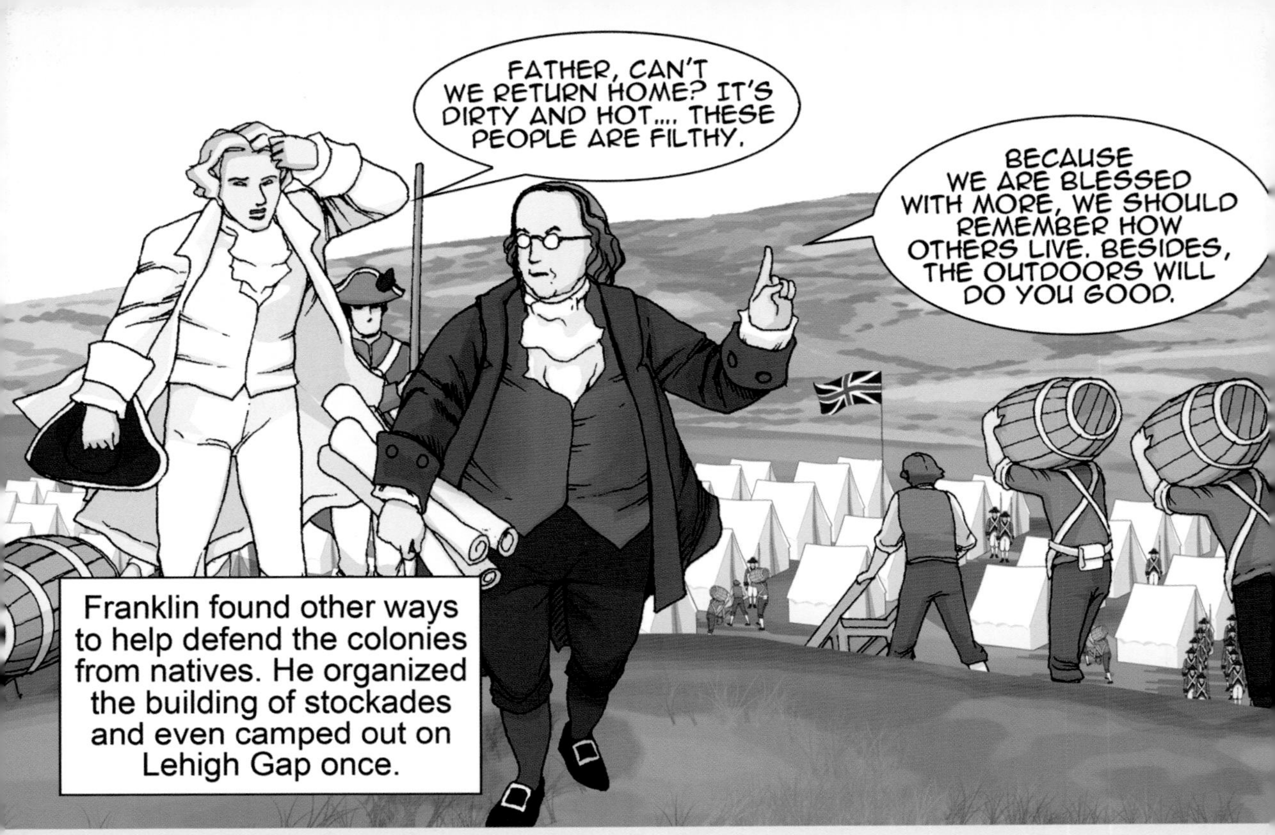
FATHER, CAN'T WE RETURN HOME? IT'S DIRTY AND HOT.... THESE PEOPLE ARE FILTHY.
BECAUSE WE ARE BLESSED WITH MORE, WE SHOULD REMEMBER HOW OTHERS LIVE. BESIDES, THE OUTDOORS WILL DO YOU GOOD.
Franklin found other ways to help defend the colonies from natives. He organized the building of stockades and even camped out on Lehigh Gap once.

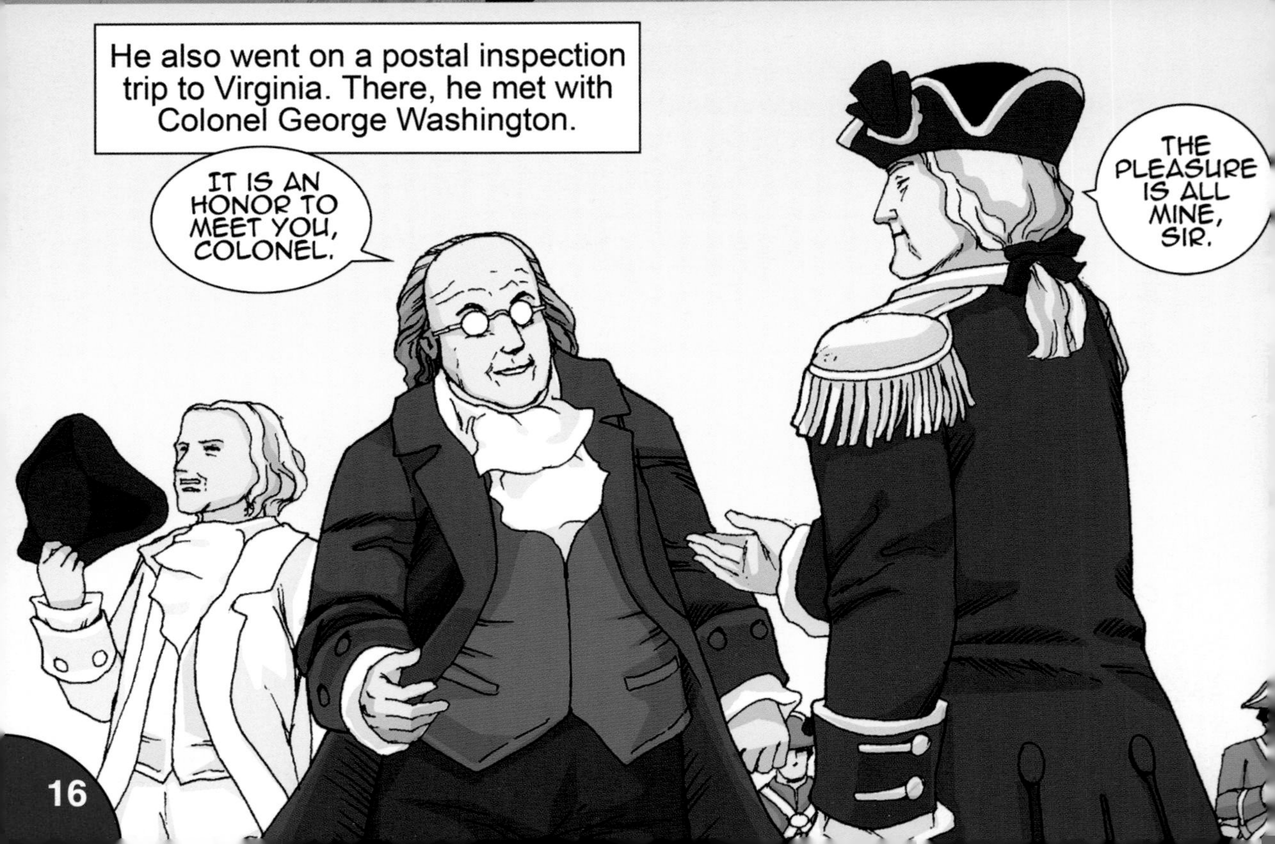
He also went on a postal inspection trip to Virginia. There, he met with Colonel George Washington.
IT IS AN HONOR TO MEET YOU, COLONEL.
THE PLEASURE IS ALL MINE, SIR.

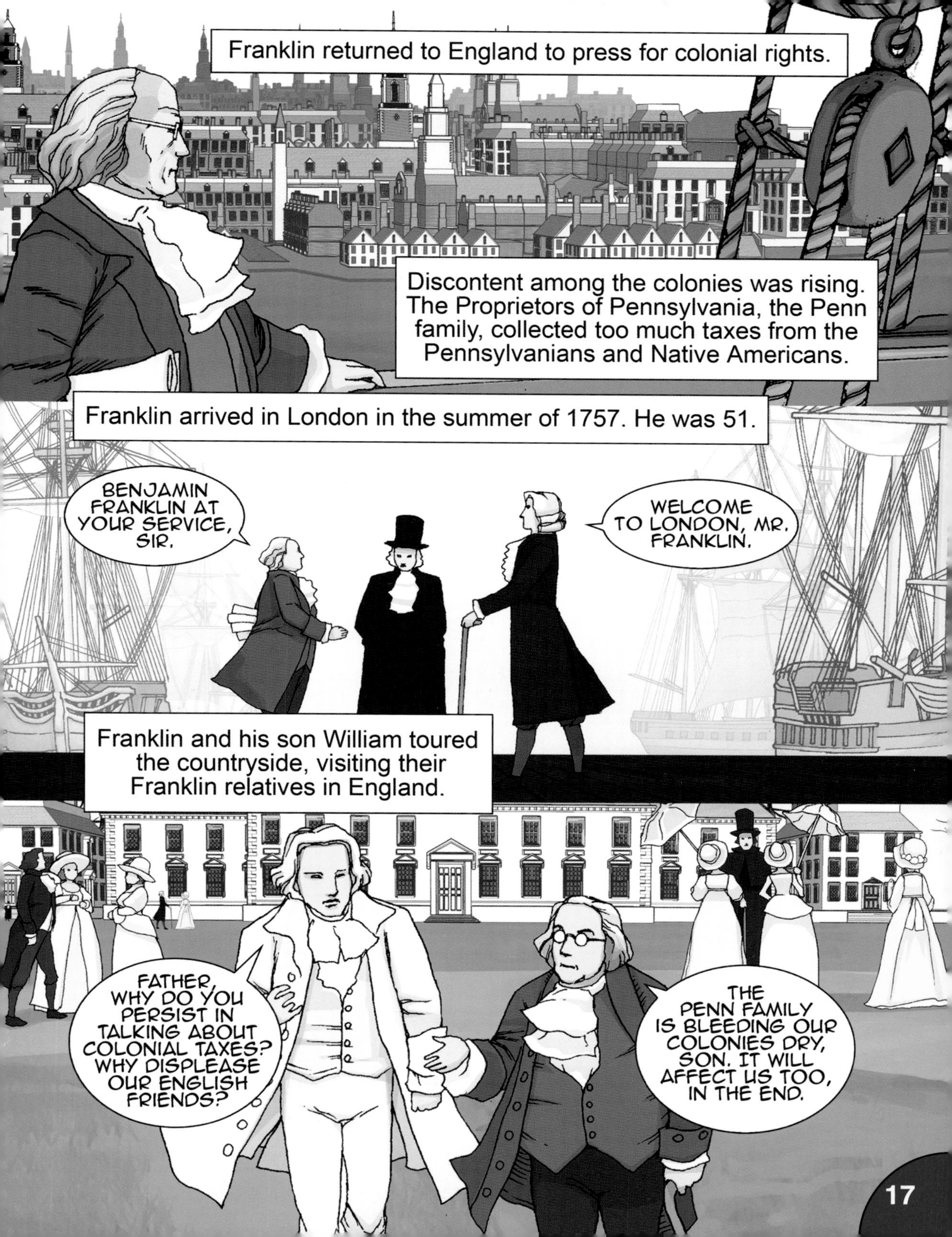
Franklin returned to England to press for colonial rights.
Discontent among the colonies was rising. The Proprietors of Pennsylvania, the Penn family, collected too much taxes from the Pennsylvanians and Native Americans.
Franklin arrived in London in the summer of 1757. He was 51.
BENJAMIN FRANKLIN AT YOUR SERVICE, SIR.
WELCOME TO LONDON, MR. FRANKLIN.
Franklin and his son William toured the countryside, visiting their Franklin relatives in England.
FATHER, WHY DO YOU PERSIST IN TALKING ABOUT COLONIAL TAXES? WHY DISPLEASE OUR ENGLISH FRIENDS?
THE PENN FAMILY IS BLEEDING OUR COLONIES DRY, SON. IT WILL AFFECT US TOO, IN THE END.

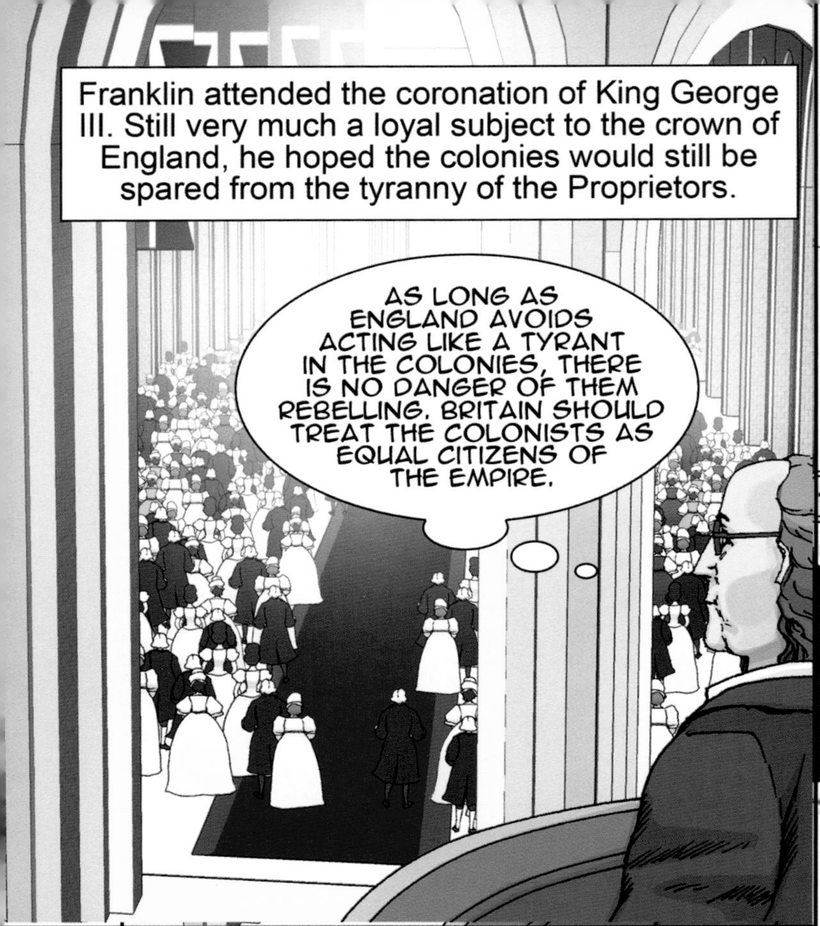
Franklin attended the coronation of King George III. Still very much a loyal subject to the crown of England, he hoped the colonies would still be spared from the tyranny of the Proprietors.
AS LONG AS ENGLAND AVOIDS ACTING LIKE A TYRANT IN THE COLONIES, THERE IS NO DANGER OF THEM REBELLING. BRITAIN SHOULD TREAT THE COLONISTS AS EQUAL CITIZENS OF THE EMPIRE.

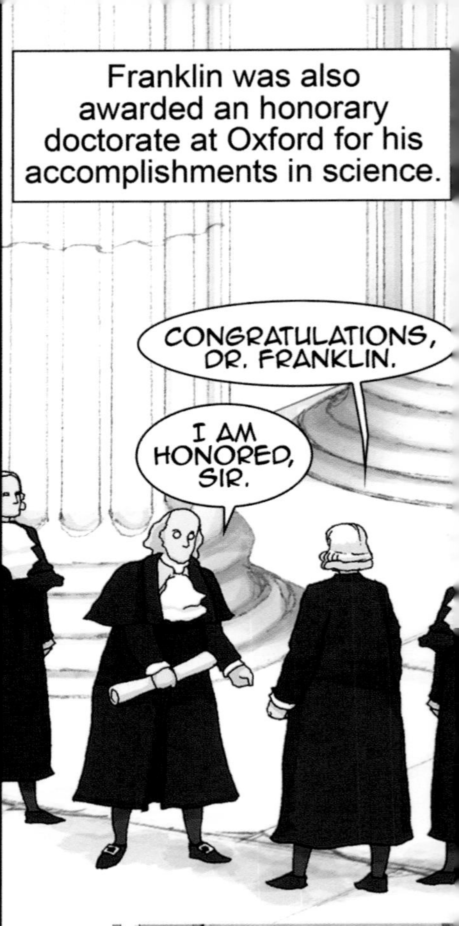
Franklin was also awarded an honorary doctorate at Oxford for his accomplishments in science.
CONGRATULATIONS, DR. FRANKLIN.
I AM HONORED, SIR.

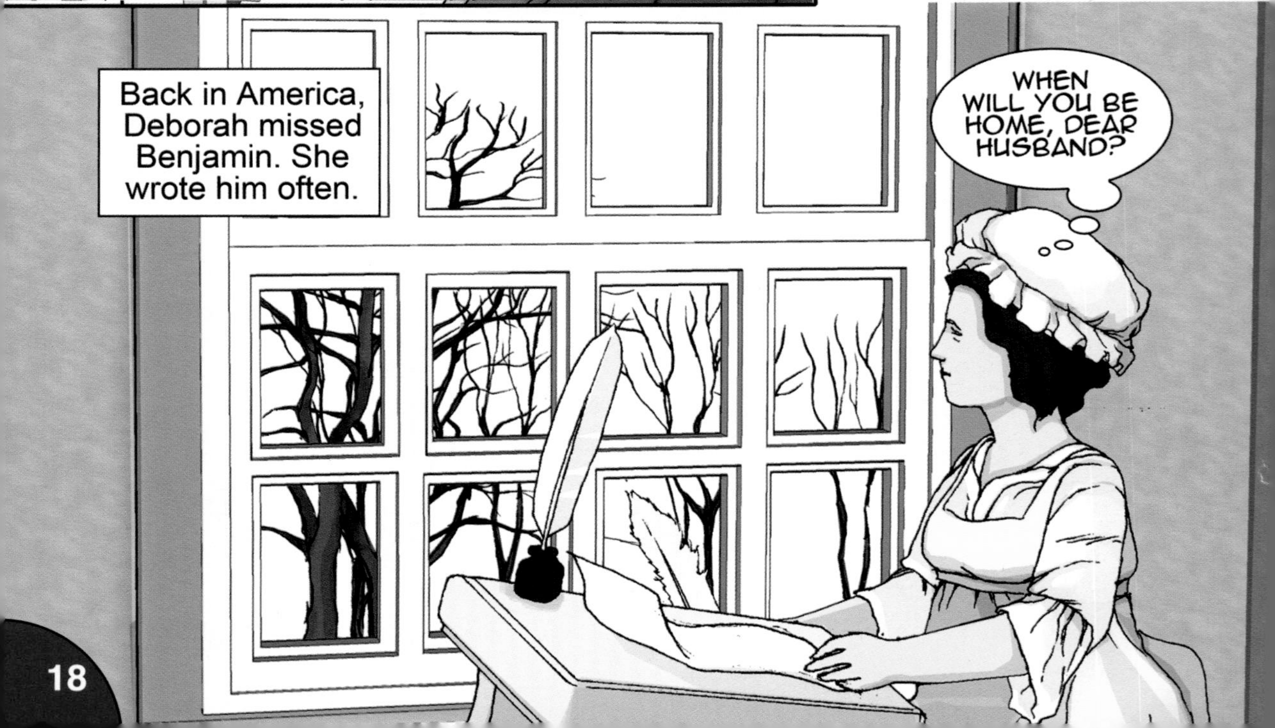
Back in America, Deborah missed Benjamin. She wrote him often.
WHEN WILL YOU BE HOME, DEAR HUSBAND?

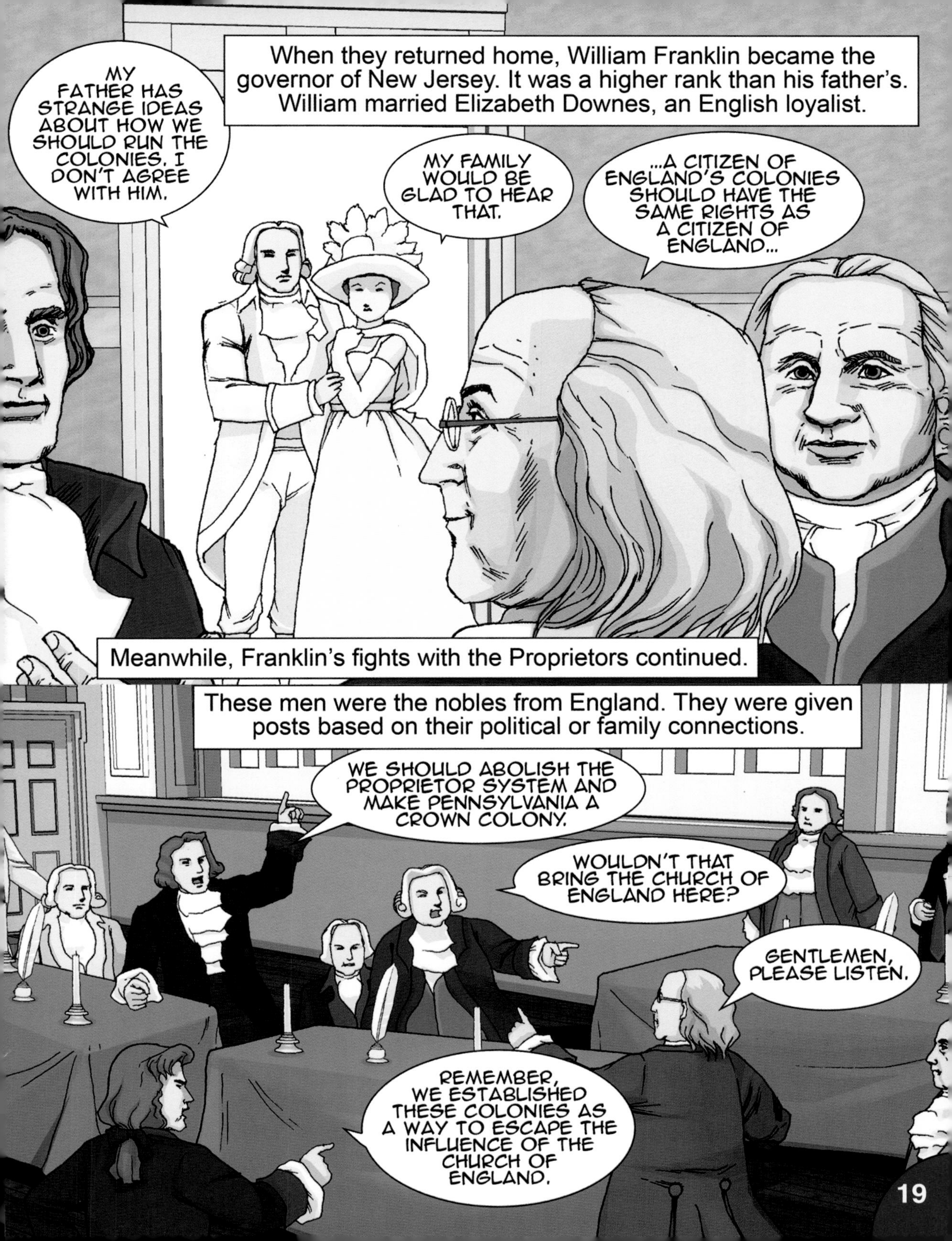

When they returned home, William Franklin became the governor of New Jersey. It was a higher rank than his father's. William married Elizabeth Downes, an English loyalist.
MY FATHER HAS STRANGE IDEAS ABOUT HOW WE SHOULD RUN THE COLONIES. I DON'T AGREE WITH HIM.
MY FAMILY WOULD BE GLAD TO HEAR THAT.
...A CITIZEN OF ENGLAND'S COLONIES SHOULD HAVE THE SAME RIGHTS AS A CITIZEN OF ENGLAND...
Meanwhile, Franklin's fights with the Proprietors continued.
These men were the nobles from England. They were given posts based on their political or family connections.
WE SHOULD ABOLISH THE PROPRIETOR SYSTEM AND MAKE PENNSYLVANIA A CROWN COLONY.
WOULDN'T THAT BRING THE CHURCH OF ENGLAND HERE?
GENTLEMEN, PLEASE LISTEN.
REMEMBER, WE ESTABLISHED THESE COLONIES AS A WAY TO ESCAPE THE INFLUENCE OF THE CHURCH OF ENGLAND.

Chapter 4 Peacemaking

Soon, Britain passed the Stamp Act. It was a tax on all printed material including books, tickets, and playing cards. While Franklin did not like the idea, his willingness to go along with it to please the British upset many in America.

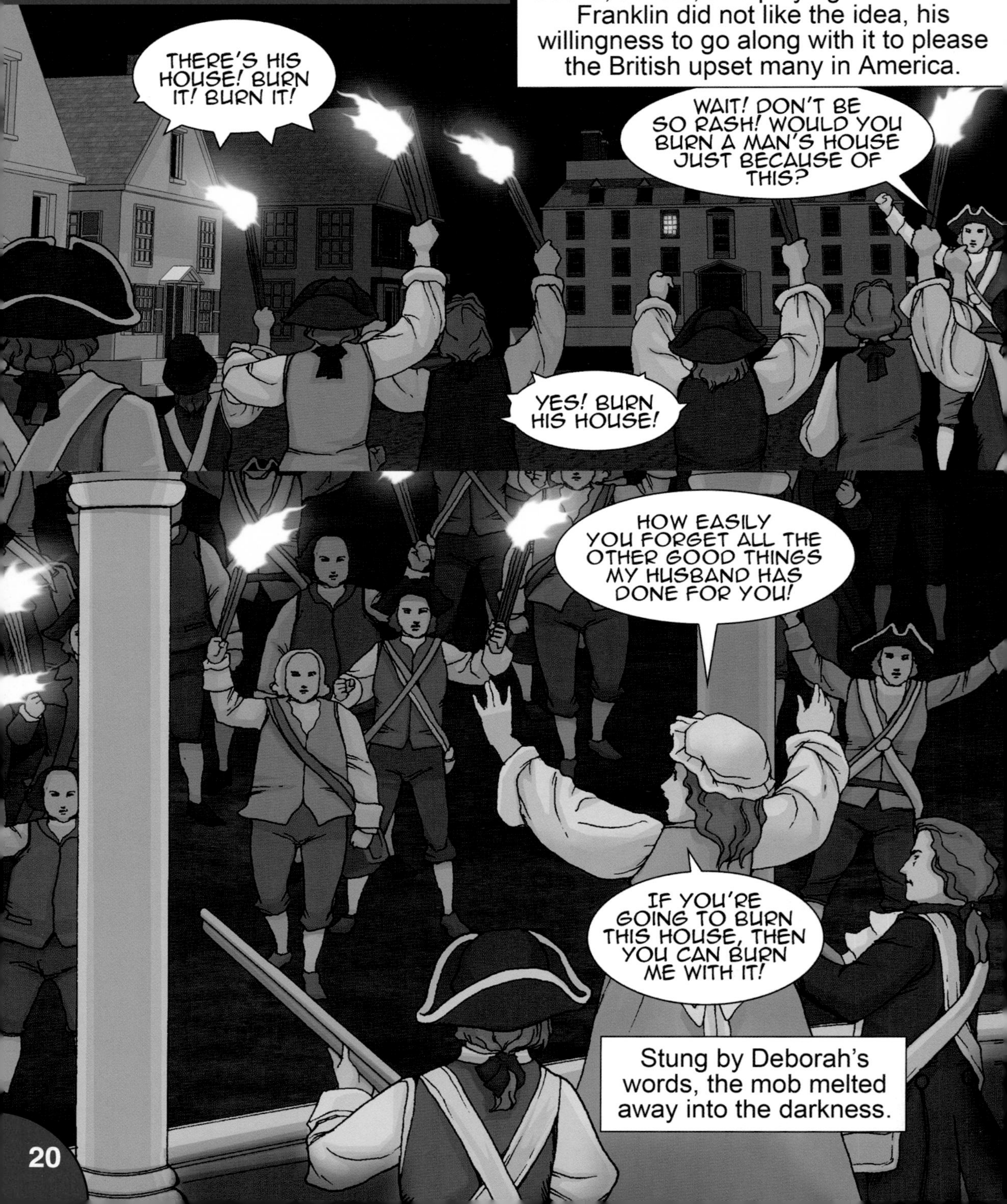

THERE'S HIS HOUSE! BURN IT! BURN IT!
WAIT! DON'T BE SO RASH! WOULD YOU BURN A MAN'S HOUSE JUST BECAUSE OF THIS?
YES! BURN HIS HOUSE!
HOW EASILY YOU FORGET ALL THE OTHER GOOD THINGS MY HUSBAND HAS DONE FOR YOU!
IF YOU'RE GOING TO BURN THIS HOUSE, THEN YOU CAN BURN ME WITH IT!

Stung by Deborah's words, the mob melted away into the darkness.

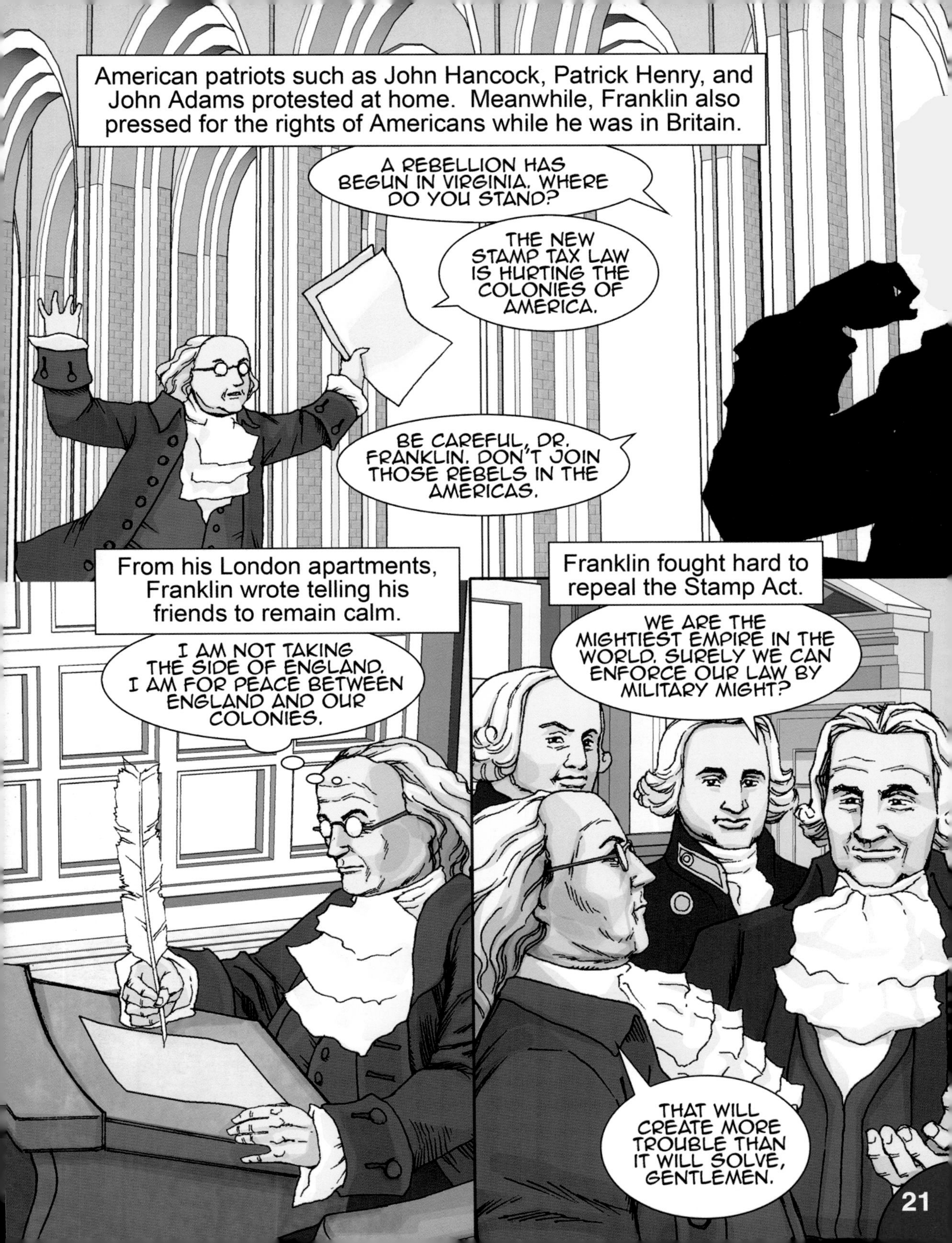

American patriots such as John Hancock, Patrick Henry, and John Adams protested at home. Meanwhile, Franklin also pressed for the rights of Americans while he was in Britain.
A REBELLION HAS BEGUN IN VIRGINIA. WHERE DO YOU STAND?
THE NEW STAMP TAX LAW IS HURTING THE COLONIES OF AMERICA.
BE CAREFUL, DR. FRANKLIN. DON'T JOIN THOSE REBELS IN THE AMERICAS.
From his London apartments, Franklin wrote telling his friends to remain calm.
I AM NOT TAKING THE SIDE OF ENGLAND. I AM FOR PEACE BETWEEN ENGLAND AND OUR COLONIES.
Franklin fought hard to repeal the Stamp Act.
WE ARE THE MIGHTIEST EMPIRE IN THE WORLD. SURELY WE CAN ENFORCE OUR LAW BY MILITARY MIGHT?
THAT WILL CREATE MORE TROUBLE THAN IT WILL SOLVE, GENTLEMEN.

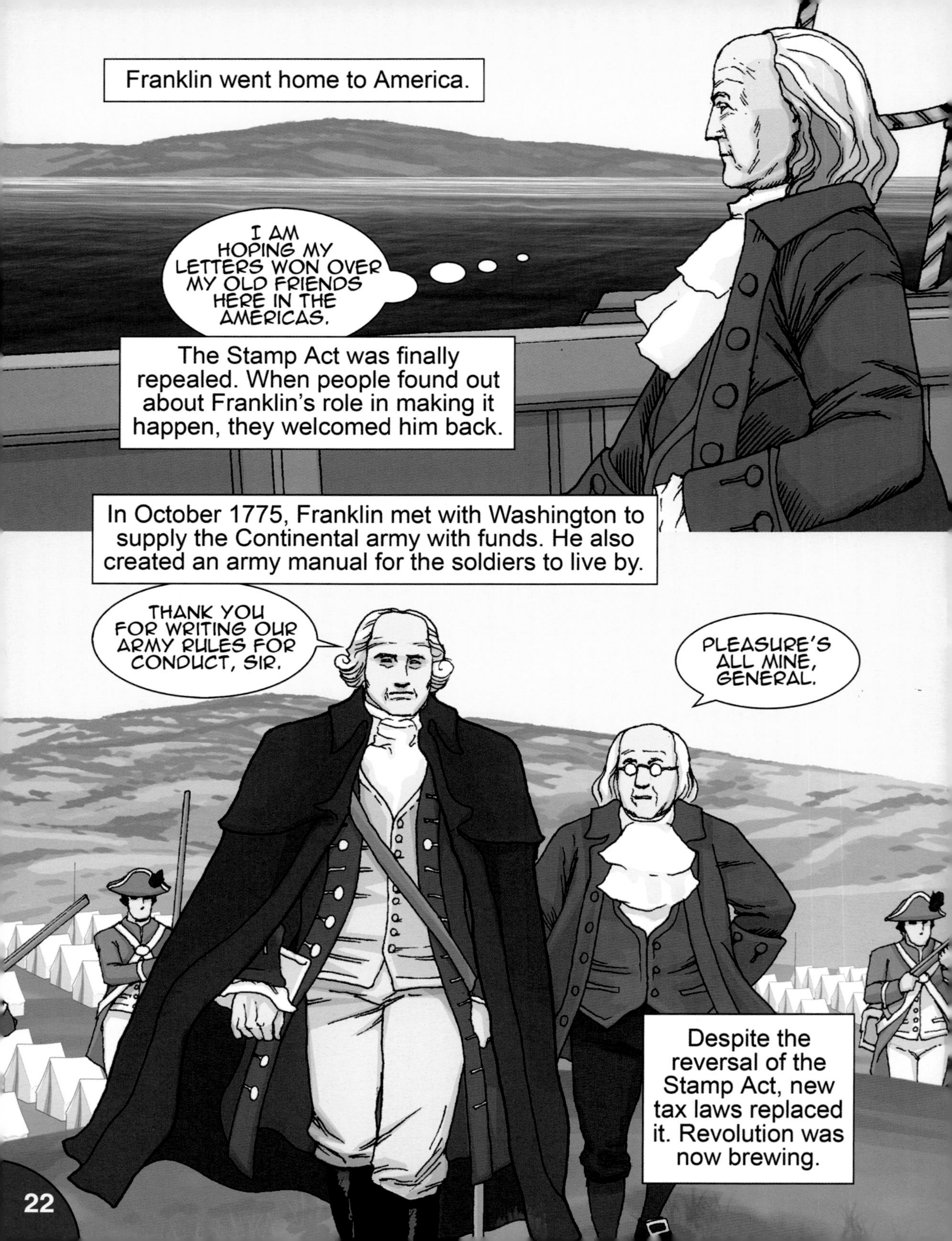
Franklin went home to America.
I AM HOPING MY LETTERS WON OVER MY OLD FRIENDS HERE IN THE AMERICAS.
The Stamp Act was finally repealed. When people found out about Franklin's role in making it happen, they welcomed him back.
In October 1775, Franklin met with Washington to supply the Continental army with funds. He also created an army manual for the soldiers to live by.
THANK YOU FOR WRITING OUR ARMY RULES FOR CONDUCT, SIR.
PLEASURE'S ALL MINE, GENERAL.
Despite the reversal of the Stamp Act, new tax laws replaced it. Revolution was now brewing.

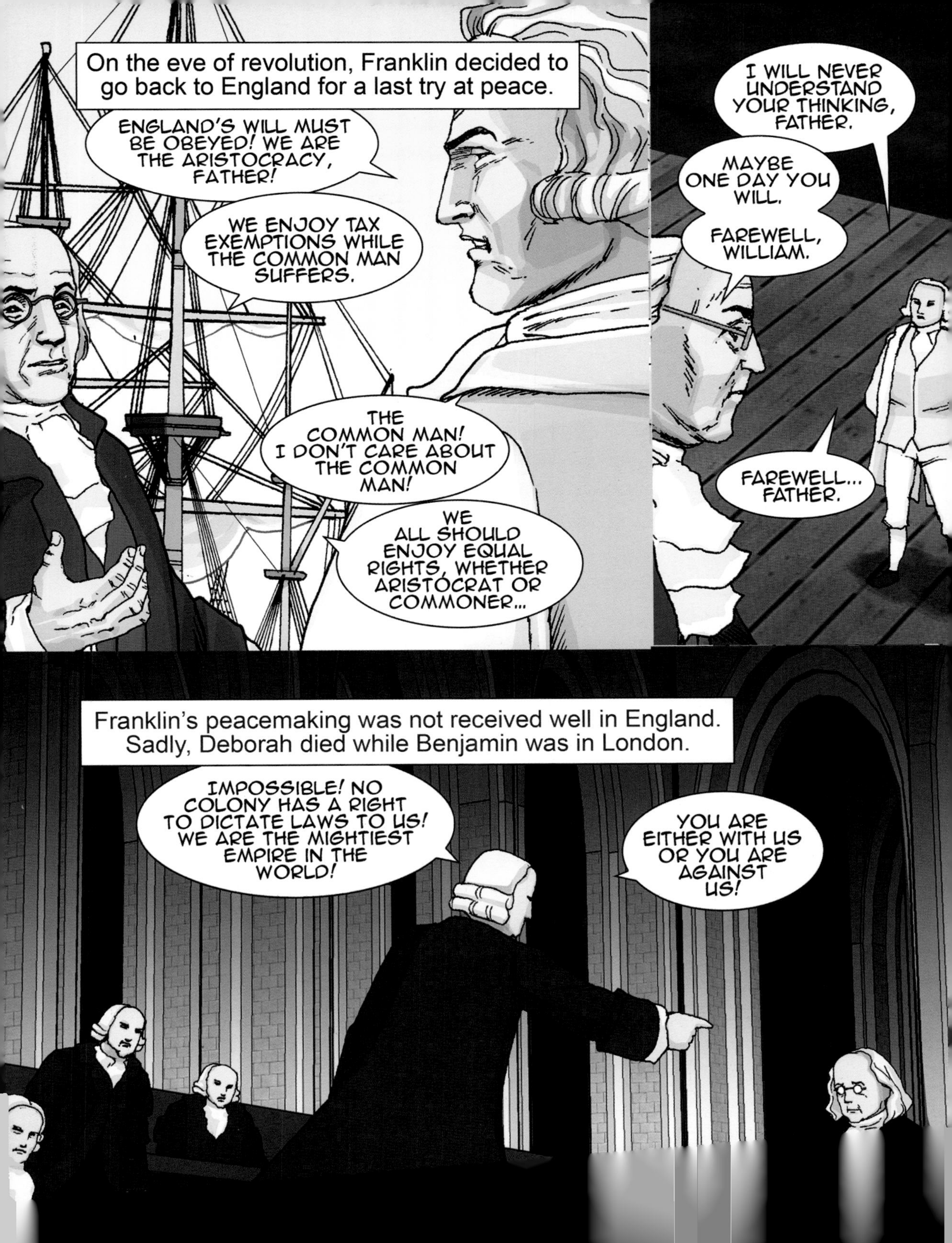
On the eve of revolution, Franklin decided to go back to England for a last try at peace.
ENGLAND'S WILL MUST BE OBEYED! WE ARE THE ARISTOCRACY, FATHER!
WE ENJOY TAX EXEMPTIONS WHILE THE COMMON MAN SUFFERS.
THE COMMON MAN! I DON'T CARE ABOUT THE COMMON MAN!
WE ALL SHOULD ENJOY EQUAL RIGHTS, WHETHER ARISTOCRAT OR COMMONER...
I WILL NEVER UNDERSTAND YOUR THINKING, FATHER.
MAYBE ONE DAY YOU WILL.
FAREWELL, WILLIAM.
FAREWELL... FATHER.
Franklin's peacemaking was not received well in England. Sadly, Deborah died while Benjamin was in London.
IMPOSSIBLE! NO COLONY HAS A RIGHT TO DICTATE LAWS TO US! WE ARE THE MIGHTIEST EMPIRE IN THE WORLD!
YOU ARE EITHER WITH US OR YOU ARE AGAINST US!

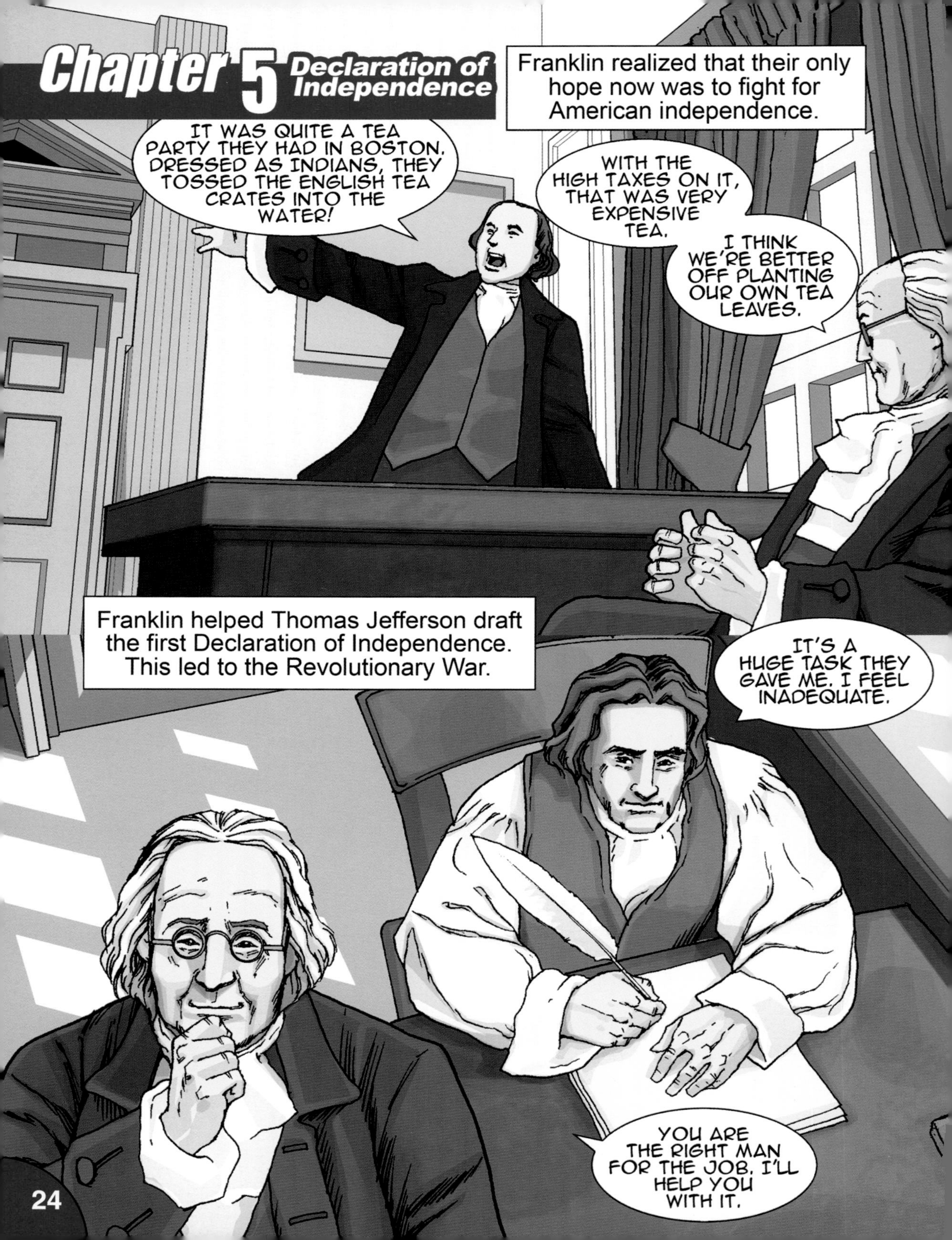
Chapter 5 Declaration of Independence
Franklin realized that their only hope now was to fight for American independence.
IT WAS QUITE A TEA PARTY THEY HAD IN BOSTON. DRESSED AS INDIANS, THEY TOSSED THE ENGLISH TEA CRATES INTO THE WATER!
WITH THE HIGH TAXES ON IT, THAT WAS VERY EXPENSIVE TEA.
I THINK WE'RE BETTER OFF PLANTING OUR OWN TEA LEAVES.
Franklin helped Thomas Jefferson draft the first Declaration of Independence. This led to the Revolutionary War.
IT'S A HUGE TASK THEY GAVE ME. I FEEL INADEQUATE.
YOU ARE THE RIGHT MAN FOR THE JOB. I'LL HELP YOU WITH IT.

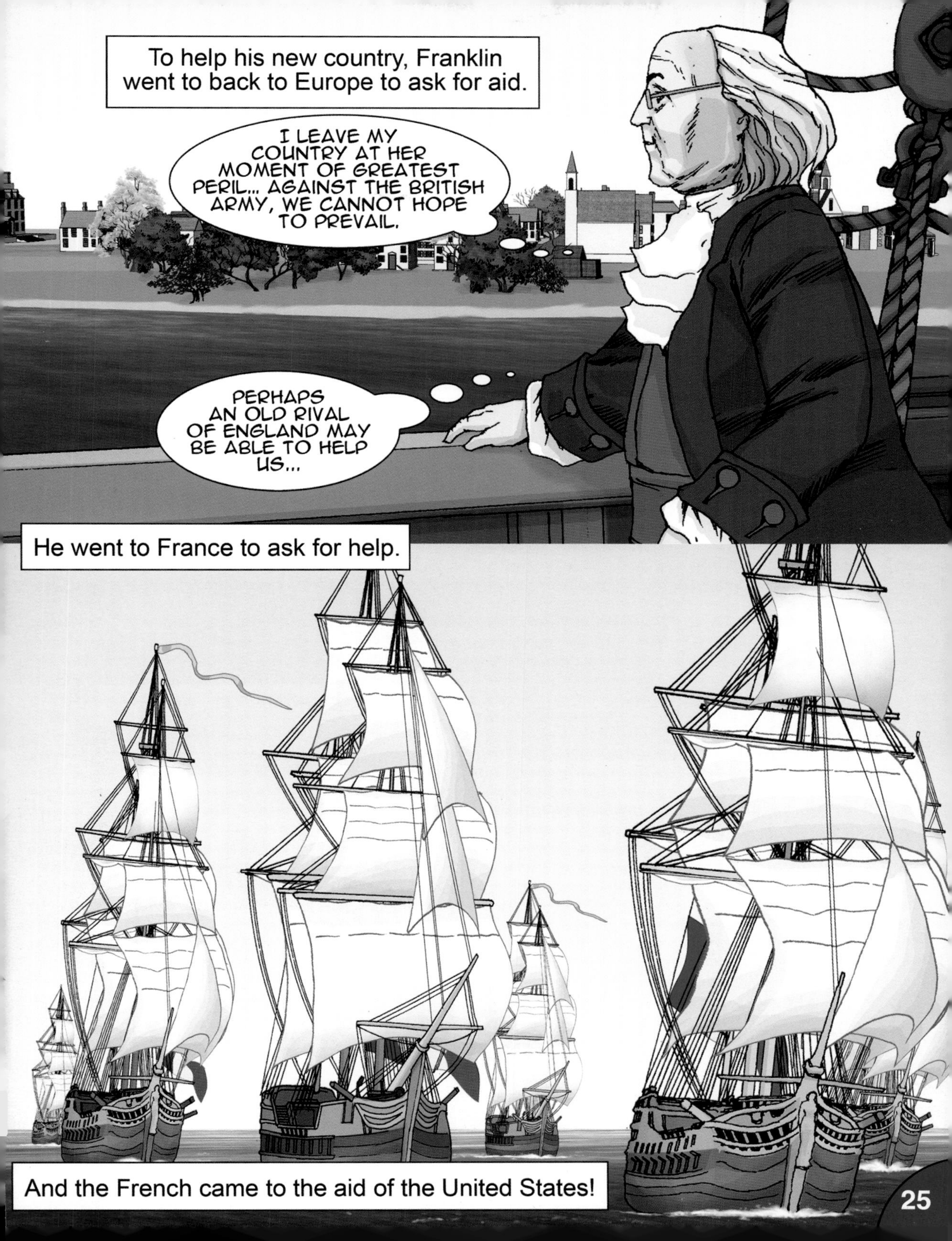
To help his new country, Franklin went to back to Europe to ask for aid.
I LEAVE MY COUNTRY AT HER MOMENT OF GREATEST PERIL... AGAINST THE BRITISH ARMY, WE CANNOT HOPE TO PREVAIL.
PERHAPS AN OLD RIVAL OF ENGLAND MAY BE ABLE TO HELP US...
He went to France to ask for help.
And the French came to the aid of the United States!

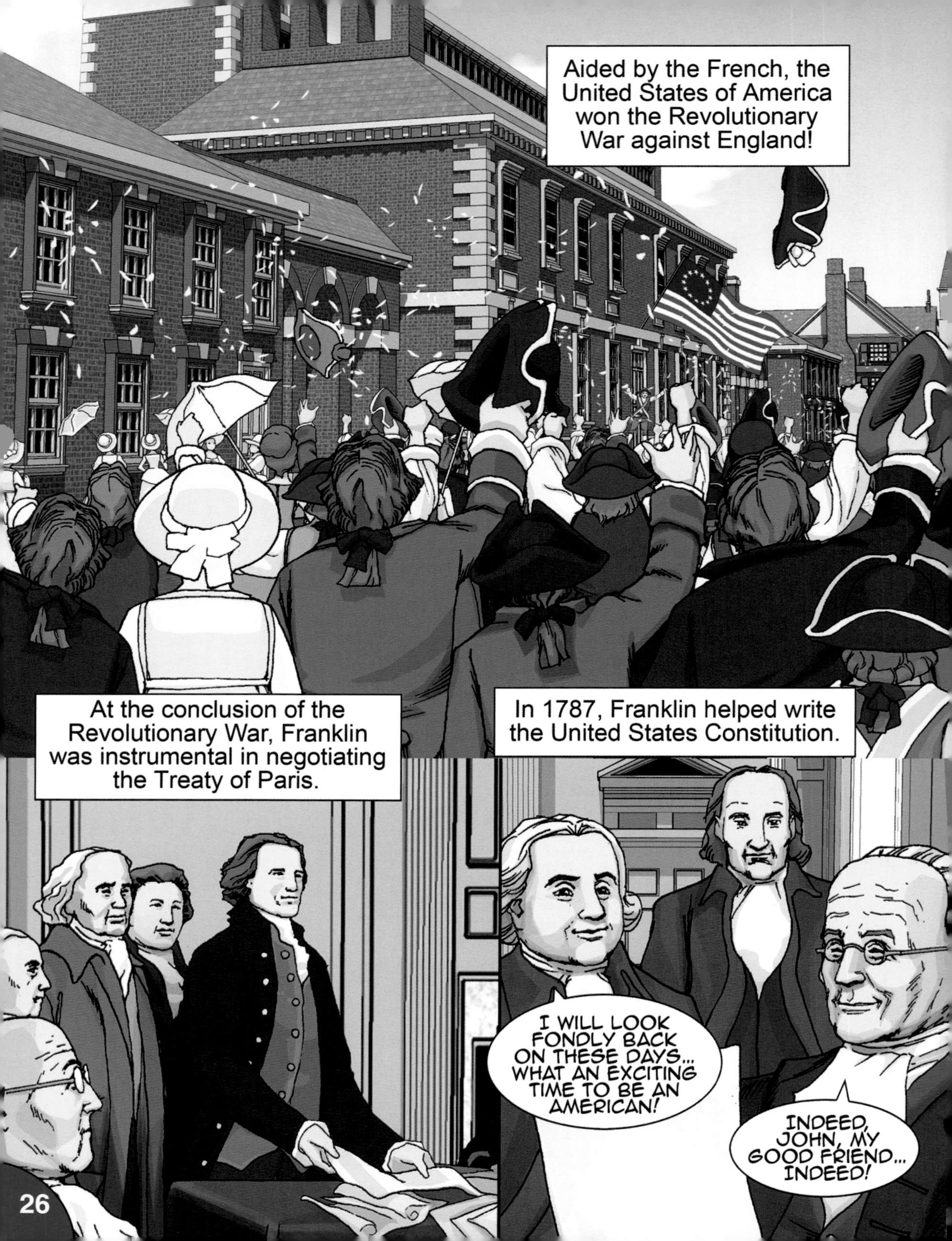
Aided by the French, the United States of America won the Revolutionary War against England!
At the conclusion of the Revolutionary War, Franklin was instrumental in negotiating the Treaty of Paris.
In 1787, Franklin helped write the United States Constitution.
I WILL LOOK FONDLY BACK ON THESE DAYS... WHAT AN EXCITING TIME TO BE AN AMERICAN!
INDEED, JOHN, MY GOOD FRIEND... INDEED!

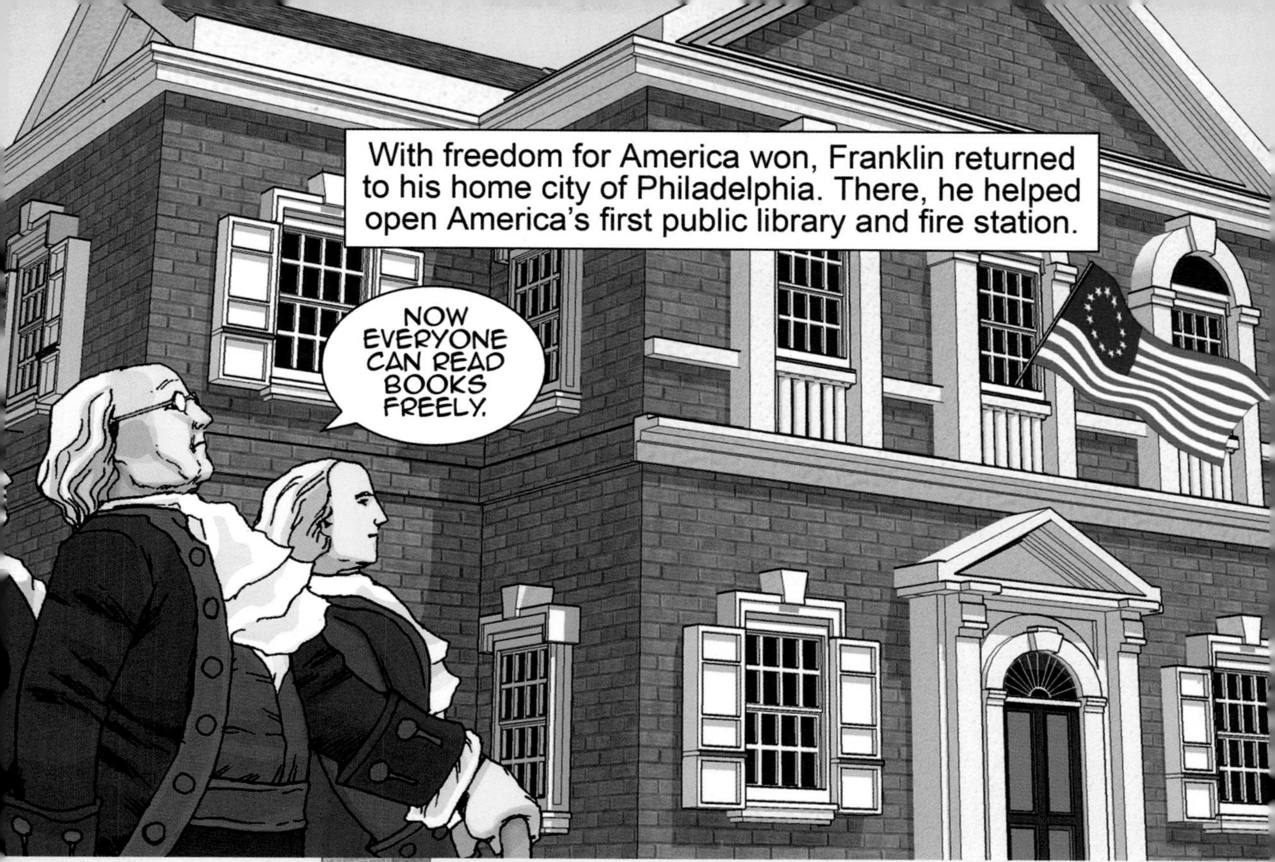
With freedom for America won, Franklin returned to his home city of Philadelphia. There, he helped open America's first public library and fire station.
NOW EVERYONE CAN READ BOOKS FREELY.

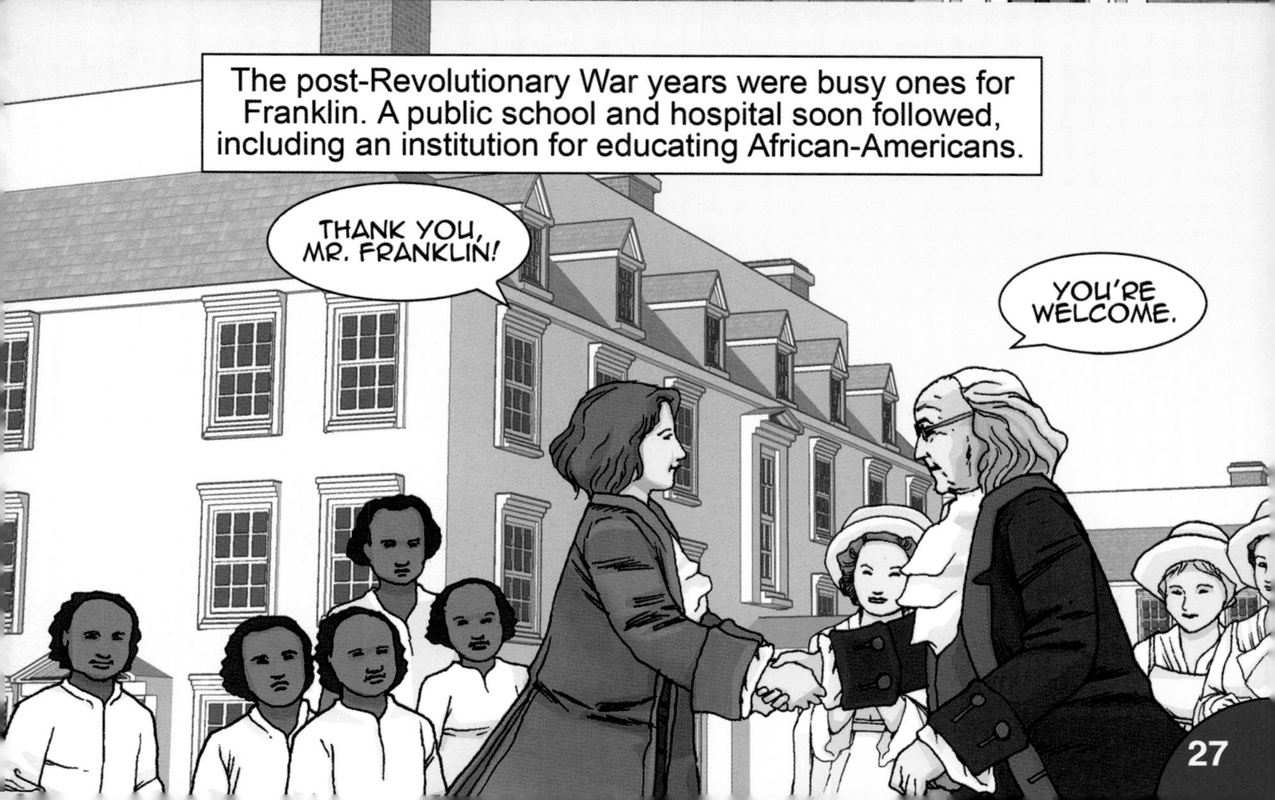
The post-Revolutionary War years were busy ones for Franklin. A public school and hospital soon followed, including an institution for educating African-Americans.
THANK YOU, MR. FRANKLIN!
YOU'RE WELCOME.

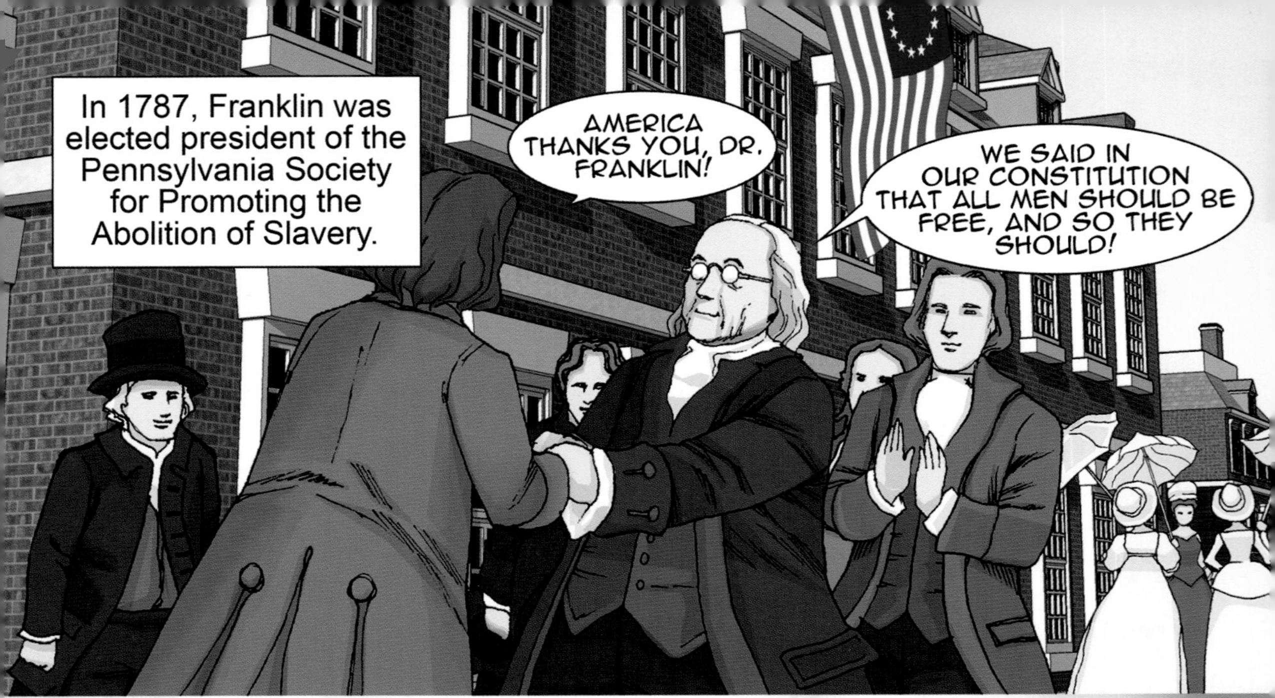
In 1787, Franklin was elected president of the Pennsylvania Society for Promoting the Abolition of Slavery.
AMERICA THANKS YOU, DR. FRANKLIN!
WE SAID IN OUR CONSTITUTION THAT ALL MEN SHOULD BE FREE, AND SO THEY SHOULD!

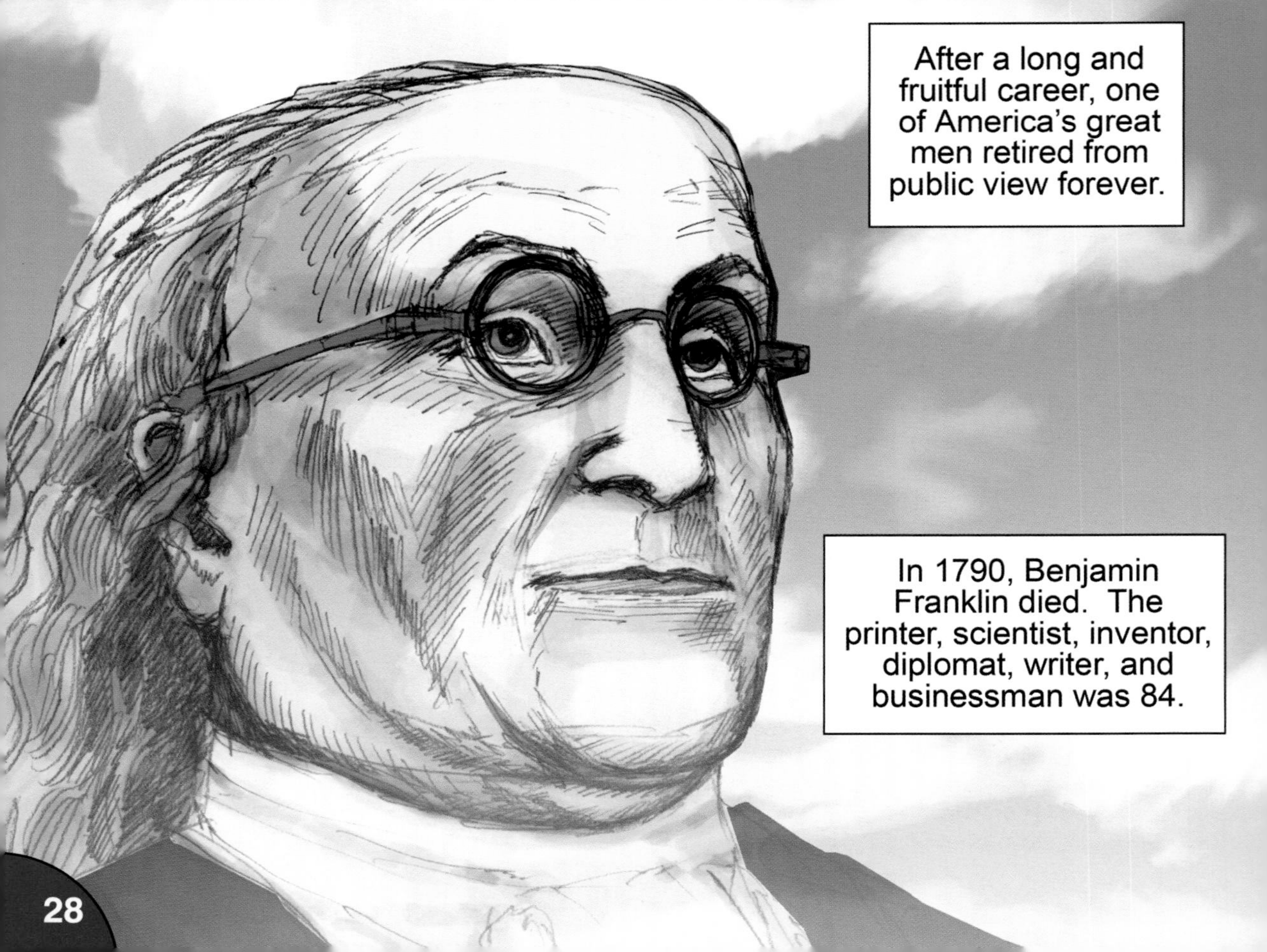
After a long and fruitful career, one of America's great men retired from public view forever.
In 1790, Benjamin Franklin died. The printer, scientist, inventor, diplomat, writer, and businessman was 84.

Timeline

1706 - Benjamin Franklin was born on January 17, in Boston, Massachusetts, to Josiah and Abiah Franklin.

1718 - Franklin was apprenticed to his brother James, who was a printer.

1729 - Franklin published *The Pennsylvania Gazette.*

1730 - Franklin married Deborah Read Rogers.

1731 - Franklin helped form the first lending library in the country.

1732 - Franklin published the first edition of the *Poor Richard's Almanack.*

1737 - Franklin was appointed Postmaster of Philadelphia.

1752 - He conducted the famous kite experiment.

1757 to 1762 - Franklin was an agent for the colonial states in England.

1775 - Franklin was elected Pennsylvania delegate of the Second Continental Congress; elected Postmaster General of the Colonies.

1776 - Franklin was one of the five men who drafted the Declaration of Independence.

1787 - Franklin signed the United States Constitution.

1789 - Franklin wrote an anti-slavery treatise.

1790 - Benjamin Franklin died in Philadelphia on April 17 at the age of 84.

Further Reading

Barrett, Gene. *Now and Ben: The Modern Inventions of Benjamin Franklin.* New York: Henry Holt, 2006.

Giblin, James Cross. *The Amazing Life of Benjamin Franklin.* New York: Scholastic Press, 2006.

Gosda, Randy T. *Benjamin Franklin.* Buddy Books First Biography. Edina: ABDO Publishing Company, 2002.

Kallen, Stuart A. *Benjamin Franklin.* Founding Fathers. Edina: ABDO Publishing Company, 2001.

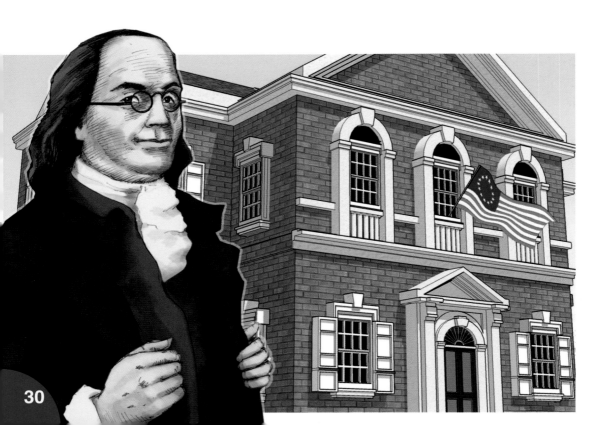

Glossary

aristocrat - a person who is born into a high social class. Aristocrats run the government in some countries.

Declaration of Independence - an essay written at the Second Continental Congress in 1776, announcing the separation of the American colonies from England.

diplomat - a person who handles the discussions and compromises between nations.

indenture - a contract that requires a person to work for another person for a stated time period.

patent - an official document giving a person the right or privilege to perform an act or a duty.

Revolutionary War - from 1775 to 1783. A war for independence between Great Britain and its North American colonies. The colonists won and created the United States of America.

tyranny - a government where one person has absolute power. The person in power is called a tyrant.

Web Sites

To learn more about Benjamin Franklin, visit ABDO Publishing Company on the World Wide Web at **www.abdopublishing.com.** Web sites about Franklin are featured on our Book Links page. These links are routinely monitored and updated to provide the most current information available.

Index